Understanding Phrasal Verbs

M. J. Murphy

Hulton Educational

First published in Great Britain 1983
by Hulton Educational Publications Ltd
Raans Road, Amersham, Bucks HP6 6JJ

ISBN 0 7175 1011 5

Printed in Great Britain by
Richard Clay (The Chaucer Press) Ltd, Bungay, Suffolk

Contents

Introduction

Phrasal verbs are very common both in spoken and written English. They are very difficult for learners of English mainly because one phrasal verb can often have a number of meanings, because the words that make up the phrasal verb are frequently not very good clues to its meaning, and because many phrasal verbs are used figuratively.

Phrasal verbs add a great deal to the force, colour and flexibility of the English language and, if a learner's vocabulary and use of English is not always to appear 'foreign', it is essential that he or she master a large number of these verbs.

Phrasal verbs are so numerous, so various and so difficult that learners too often tend to avoid them if they can. In this book an attempt has been made to bring some order into this confusion by grouping phrasal verbs into certain categories. It must be understood, however, that while a great number of phrasal verbs fall into these categories, not all of them do.

Learners who work their way through this book will have a greater understanding of the English phrasal verb and its uses and should be able more easily to understand new phrasal verbs when they meet them.

How to use this book

This book can be used in two ways: (1) as a self-study book and (2) it can be used by a teacher as a class book to supplement and add variety to an everyday basic English course.

1 There are as many ways of self-study as there are people but here are a few hints.

(a) Go through the examples carefully several times. Before going on to the exercises try to make up other sentences using these verbs. (b) Work your way through the exercises. (c) In the exercises in which you are asked to use phrasal verbs freely in response to questions, try to imagine a situation and try to say as much as you can about it. Use your imagination; let it wander. Use phrasal verbs from previous sections of the book or any others that you know. (d) To acquire a stock of these verbs and to reinforce those you have already learnt, look out for them in the speech of native speakers and in the novels and newspapers you may read. (e) Once you have acquired a phrasal verb, practise using it as much as you can in your speech and writing. Remember that, although some phrasal verbs are marked as collo-quial, they can still be used in writing depending on what you wish to say, how you wish to say it and to whom you wish to say it. (f) Keep lists of phrasal verbs you come across under the various categories in this book. Remember that all phrasal verbs do not fall within these categories, so keep a miscellaneous list as well.

2 Again there are as many ways of using this book as there are teachers. But here are a few hints. (a) Work through the examples with the students. Do a few at a time. (b) Get the students to make up other sentences using these verbs as you go along. (c) Think up any other activities you can to reinforce their use e.g. act out some phrasal verbs. (For example, write a word on the blackboard and rub it out. Ask students what you have done.) Try to elicit the verb: *to rub out.* You could also get the students to act out verbs. (d) The exercises can be done in class or as homework exercises. Where there are alternatives discuss them if possible. Are there any differences? Try to choose the most suitable. (e) Set an example yourself. Use phrasal verbs in your own speech wherever possible. (f) In the exer-cises in which the students are required to give free answers, encour-age them to use their imaginations. It is a good idea to have them work in pairs or fours. To help them at first you may write lists of verbs suitable for use in their answers on the board. Or you may prepare cards with suitable verbs written on them. (g) Always try to bring out the difference between the romance/latinate verb and the phrasal verb e.g. between pairs such as: *to put out/extinguish; to pull out/extract; to throw out/expel; to put in/insert; to go on/proceed; to die away/diminish; to blow up/inflate* etc. The phrasal verb is, as a general rule, less formal, less technical or scientific, more forceful and more colourful.

Note that there are more than ten phrasal verbs used in this introduction!

Abbreviations used

coll. Colloquial, most commonly used in speech between friends and family. This does not mean, however, that its use is restricted to spoken English.

fig. The verb is used in a figurative sense.

Note

For the purpose of this book, I have made no distinction between:
prepositional verbs (verb + preposition);
phrasal verbs (verb + particle)
prepositional-phrasal verbs (verb + two particles).
These definitions do not help the student to decide on correct usage. Therefore I have used the 'umbrella' name – 'phrasal verb' to describe all the above.

In the same way, I have used 'preposition/particle' throughout as the student is not concerned with the distinction between the two when he or she is trying to decide on meaning; context will then usually be the deciding factor.

1 Particles with verbs of motion

The simplest use of particles is with verbs of motion when the particle has a directional sense — i.e. it expresses direction.

a The particles commonly used with verbs of motion in this sense are **in, out, down, off, on, away, over, (a)round, about, through, back, along, across, past, by**

The water's warm — *dive in.*/ The car door opened and a small girl *jumped out.*/ It took us an hour to *climb up* here. I hope it doesn't take us as long to *walk down.*/ The actor bowed in the centre of the stage and then *walked off.*/ The director of the play said, 'When you *walk on*, hold your hands like this.'/ When the dog *came up* to him the boy *backed away.*/ We'll *drive over* and see you this afternoon./ In the restaurant John *came over* to our table and asked us to join him./ I'll *come round* tonight and help you with your homework./ I didn't have time to visit you when I was in London, I was just *passing through.*/ The policeman said to the crowd, '*Move back*, please.'/ There's not much room on this bench — will you *shift along* a little please./ 'When did you come back from France?' 'Oh, I *flew across* (fig) this morning.' When I spoke to the man he just *turned round* and *walked away.*/ I watched the traffic *speeding past.*/ I thought I saw your brother *pass by.*

b The verb **get** when being used as a verb of motion can be used with all these particles.

When the bus stopped some passengers *got in* and others *got out.*/ The river was in flood and they couldn't *get across.*/ The train's stopped — it's time to *get off.*/ I didn't know you were home. When did you *get back*?

c **Up** in the directional sense often conveys the meaning of *coming very close to*. **Up** can also be used with **to**.

A messenger *walked up* and spoke in the Prime Minister's ear./ The aeroplane *taxied up* to the edge of the tarmac.

Exercises

1 *Put a suitable directional particle in each space.*

1 When I called to him he turned . . . . . . and saw me.
2 Because the propeller was damaged the ship had to go . . . . . . to port.
3 Throw that dead mouse . . . . . ! The cat must have dragged it . . . .
4 The door opened and an old man came . . . . He walked to the edge of the pavement and stood and watched the traffic racing . . . . Then he shrugged his shoulders, turned . . . . . . and went into the house again.
5 As I was sitting in the park a small girl walked . . . . . . and said she was lost.
6 On these cold winter mornings I like my bed. It's all I can do to crawl . . . .
7 'Hello George, I didn't expect to see you.' 'Oh, I was passing . . . . . . and I thought I would just call . . . . . . for a minute.'
8 The policeman said to the crowd gathered near the accident, 'Come on now, move . . . . . ; you're holding up the traffic.'
9 John you need a holiday. You must go . . . . . . for a few weeks.
10 You know where our house is. If you are driving . . . . . . at any time, please drop . . . . . . and have a drink and a chat.

2 *In each sentence below put a* **phrasal verb** *which means the opposite of the one in italics.*

1 'John, go upstairs and get my umbrella.' 'Oh, I've just *come down*. Do I have to . . . . . . again?'
2 'We're *driving up* to Scotland next week and the week after, we're . . . . . . to the south of England.'
3 The manager called his secretary into his office. She looked cheerful enough when she . . . . . . but not so cheerful when she *came out*.
4 When the girl had an argument with her parents she *ran away* from home but a week later she . . . .

8

5 The piston in a car engine *moves up* the cylinder to the top of its stroke and then it . . . . . .

6 There was a lot of activity at number 7 Oak Street this morning. As one family was . . . . . . another family was *moving out*.

3 *Put a suitable verb from this list with a suitable* **directional particle** *in each space below. There may be alternatives — discuss these. Make sure the verb is in a suitable form.*

bring, climb, come, drive, fall, hurry, jump, move, pass, run, travel, walk, get,

1 The little boy was running when he . . . . . . and hit his head on a stone.

2 The old man sat in the park and watched the people . . . .

3 There's a cat at the top of that lamp post. How ever did it . . . . . . that high?

4 The old man sits there and no one ever talks to him. They all just . . . .

5 I have some books for you at home. I'll . . . . . . them . . . . . . this evening.

6 The stream is not very wide. I'm sure you can . . . .

7 The man was very weak after his illness and when he tried to stand he . . . . . . on to his bed.

8 As the detective was watching the house he saw a large car *drive* . . and stop right in front of it.

9 When the dog growled at him the small boy . . . . . . in fright.

10 The girl who forgot her lines in the play was so embarrassed that she turned and . . . .

11 The lorry stopped and a young man on the back said to the hitchhiker, '. . . . . . quick.'

12 'We're late because there was a traffic jam and we couldn't . . . .'

4 *Imagine yourself in each of the situations described below. Write down what you would say, using a verb of motion with a directional particle.*

1 You have just opened the door of your house and a friend is standing there. Invite him to enter.

2 Your brother has come into your room and is annoying you. Order him angrily to leave.

3 You have had an argument with your boyfriend/girlfriend. Order him/her to leave you and never to return.
4 A friend has asked you for the loan of a book you value. Tell him he can take it with him but he must return it.
5 A friend has just come to visit you. Tell him you are sorry, you are just leaving the house but you will return in about an hour.

2

Particles with verbs implying motion: part 1

The common particles used with verbs of motion are
in, back, out, up, down, away, over

a to be

Wait for me. I'll *be out* in a moment./ I'll *be back* in a minute./ John's upstairs — he'll *be down* in a minute.

b to put, to take

Did you *put* the cat *out*?/ She made some soup and forgot to *put* any salt *in*./ I don't want that food — *take* it *away*!/ If you want to ask a question *put* your hand *up*.

c to ask, to call, to invite, to have (i.e. invite/ask), **to order, to show, to see** (i.e. accompany), **to help, to lead**

'Mr Smith is in the outer office, sir.' 'Oh, *ask* him *in* please.'/ There's Fred. *Call* him *over*./ My mother lives in Scotland but we *invite* her *down* now and again./ That friend of yours came to the house yesterday and he just *invited* himself *back* today./ John *had* some of his old school friends *in* last night and they talked until 2 a.m./ Because of the uproar in the courtroom the judge *ordered* everyone *out*./ It's good manners to *show*/*see* your guests *out* when they are leaving./ The road's very busy. I'll *help* you *over*./ It was Billy's job as class captain to *lead* the class *in* every morning.

d To show out also has the sense of making or causing someone to leave.

This person is making a nuisance of himself in my office. *Show* him *out* please.

e to hit, to strike, to hammer, to drive (i.e. to force) **to kick, to press, to pull, to push, to screw, to suck, to breathe**

He was so angry he just *hit out* blindly and knocked his brother over./ When the thief approached me I *struck out* with my left fist./ The scout *hammered* the tent pegs *in* firmly./ *Drive* those nails *in* properly./ The enemy attack was *driven back*./ Those drinking friends of my husband's wouldn't go home last night. I had to *kick* them *out (fig)*./ The horse was frightened and he *kicked out* violently with his hind legs./ The driver *pressed/pushed* the accelerator *down* and the car shot away./ If you *pull* the lever *over* to the right the machine will start./ The bolt fell out because it hadn't been *screwed in* properly./ The little boy *sucked up* the last of his ice cream soda through his drinking straw./ The swimmer was *sucked down* by the strong current./ The doctor said, 'Breathe in slowly. Now *breathe out.*'

f to wave, to signal, to beckon

The people who were running to the scene of the accident were *waved back* by the police./ At the road block the police *signalled* me *out* because I had an official number plate./ The old lady caught the waiter's attention and *beckoned* him *over*.

Exercises

1 *In each space in each sentence below put* **either** *a suitable verb selected from those discussed above* **or** *a suitable directional particle. (There may be alternatives — discuss these).*

1 The car manufacturers must do something. No human being should have to . . . . . . in those filthy exhaust fumes that modern cars pour . . . .
2 When his guest stood . . . . . . to leave the host said that he would . . . . . . her out.
3 The old lady said, 'As far as cars are concerned, I can get . . . . . . all right but I always need someone to . . . . . . me out.'
4 Don't . . . . . . those tent pegs in too far because we'll have trouble in . . . . . . them out.
5 The swimming dog disappeared, ... down by the strong current, but he bobbed . . . . . . again a few yards away.
6 When we were . . . . . . last night at the cinema some thieves . . . . . . in and stole our television set.

7 The demonstrators had . . . . . . up a large sign up in front of the Prime Minister's residence but the police . . . . . . it down.

8 Our new neighbours moved . . . . . . a week ago. Isn't it time we had them . . . . . . for a drink?

9 When the President's car stopped one of his aides stepped . . . . . . to . . . . . . him out but the President . . . . . . him away.

10 Will you please . . . . . . this letter in to Mr Smith?

11 Mr Smith says that, if you'll kindly sit . . . . . , he'll . . . . . . out in a minute.

2 *In each space below put a phrasal verb that is the opposite, or almost the opposite, of the one in italics.*

1 He *took up* his coat and was about to leave when he found that he had . . . . . . his hat . . . . . . and couldn't find it.

2 In this exercise you *push down* with your hands against the floor and then you . . . . . . against the bar over your head.

3 The police were *sent in* to try to control the riot but when the danger of injuries on both sides increased the police chief . . . . . . them . . . . . . out.

4 The flag was *put up* in the morning and . . . . . . in the evening.

5 I . . . . . . a few friends . . . . . . for Tom's birthday but I wish I hadn't. I had to *kick* the last one *out* at 4 a.m.

6 A diner at one of the tables *beckoned* the waiter *over*, then changed his mind and . . . . . . him . . . .

7 Mary called from upstairs, 'I'll *be down* in a minute.' But Jane answered, 'Don't bother — I'll . . . .'

8 The science teacher said, 'I hold the flask like this. I *take* the stopper *out* and then I . . . . . . the acid . . . . . . carefully.

3 *Try to answer each of these questions using a phrasal verb with a directional particle.*

e.g. **Q:** *Where is the money I put in the drawer?*

   A: *I took it out this morning. (Discuss any alternatives)*

1 Why's the waiter coming to our table?

2 Why are John and Mary driving down from Scotland tomorrow to stay with us?

3 What should I do if I see a blind person waiting to cross a busy street?

4 I have a thorn in my foot. What shall I do?

5 There's a man who wants to see you, sir. What shall I tell him?

6 What would you do with guests who stayed until three in the morning?

7 As a host, what should I do when one of my guests is leaving?

8 Mary's downstairs and wants to see you. What shall I say?

3 Particles with verbs implying motion: part 2

a to let, to allow

Close the door and don't *let* the cat *in*./ John has been ill so he is not *allowed out*./ The courtroom was locked and the public were not *allowed in*./ The police formed a line in front of the embassy gate and they would not *let* anybody *through*.

b to look, to see

Draw the curtains. With the light on in the room anyone can *look/ see in*./ He opened the windows and *looked out*./ Don't *look down* when I'm talking to you./ As the runner entered the straight he *looked back* to see where the others were./ Those windows are so dirty that I can't *see out*.

c to phone, to ring

There's something wrong with our phone. People can *phone in* but we can't *phone out*.

d to send, to ship, to fly

The government said it would *send in* the army if the rebels did not lay down their arms./ That consignment of machinery for the Far East was *shipped out* yesterday./ Emergency food supplies were *flown in* for the starving refugees.

e to throw, to toss

The player *threw* the ball *in*./ He *tossed* the empty bottle *away*./ The smell of that food almost made me *throw up* (= vomit)./ John and Jim were *thrown out* (*fig.*) of Mary's party last night because they hadn't been invited.

f to force, to push, to work

These verbs can be used with **way** as an object.

I told him he could not come in but he *forced/pushed* his *way in./* These small insects attach themselves to the skin and then *work* their *way in.*

g to point, to smuggle, to pour, to break, to wash

The boy *pointed up* to the helicopter which was circling the playing field./ If you try to *smuggle* anything *in*, the customs people will catch you./ The rain was *pouring down./* The tank had a hole in it and the petrol was *pouring out./* Thieves *broke in* last night and stole a lot of money./ Some prisoners *broke out* of gaol last night./ The swimmer was *washed out* to sea by the strong current.

Exercises

1 *In each space below put* **either** *a suitable verb from those discussed above* **or** *a suitable directional particle:*

1 The class had been naughty and when the school bell rang the teacher wouldn't . . . . . . them out. First he made them stand . . . . . . and then sit . . . . Finally he said, 'Tom can go . . . . . . first and the others can follow him . . . . . . quietly.'
2 The leader of the prisoners said, 'We'll . . . . . . out tonight. The wall will be easy enough to get . . . . All we have to do is climb to the top then jump . . . . . . and we're free.'
3 When the customs officer came . . . . . . to him he tried to . . . . . . his way past. It was later found that he was trying to . . . . . . in several bars of gold.
4 He stood by his bed, stretched his arms . . . . . . and yawned. Then he walked . . . . . . to the windows and drew . . . . . . the curtains so as to . . . . . . the sunlight in. When he . . . . . . out he saw that everything was covered with snow.
5 The manager . . . . . . up at his assistant and said, 'We can't . . . . . . that consignment out this week because there's a seamen's strike. We'll have to . . . . . . it out by Singapore Airways.'
6 The lava from a volcano . . . . . . its way up from the depths of the earth. Some of it shoots . . . . . . into the air but most of it flows . . . . . . the sides of the mountain.
7 The centre-forward . . . . . . the ball in but one of the opposing team kicked it . . . . . . again.

8 The girl left the cage door open and her pet budgerigar got
. . . . . . and . . . . . . away.
9 'Any news of the prisoners who broke . . . . . . last night?' 'Yes,
a constable on his beat . . . . . . in an hour ago and said he thought
he saw them driving . . . . . . in a black car.'
10 The fat man opened his mouth, popped . . . . . . several large
oysters and . . . . . . them down with a large mouthful of beer.

2 *In each sentence below choose the correct verb from those given in brackets.*

1 For years scientists have been looking for a cure for cancer but
now they think they might be about to (point/look/fly/break)
through (*fig*).
2 'Are those old shirts of yours any good?' 'No, let's (show/throw/
send/put) them out.'
3 When the mixture of air and petrol explodes in the cylinder the
expanding gases try to (force/fly/let/pour) their way out.
4 The boy who was being very naughty during the lesson was (forced/
allowed/sent/seen) out by the teacher.
5 'I can't get this piece of glass out of my hand.' 'Well, just leave it
for a day or so and it will probably (wash/work/pour/show) itself
out.'
6 Pieces of the wrecked ship were (sent/poured/washed/sucked) up
on the beach.
7 The night-watchman of the factory (signalled/waved/ordered/
phoned) in a warning that he thought thieves were trying to (force/
look/break/push) in.
8 Some people walk with their toes (pointing/showing/flying/looking)
out like Charlie Chaplin.

3 *Try to answer each of these questions using a phrasal verb with a
directional particle.*

1 What would you think if you saw a person acting suspiciously as
he approached the customs inspection point?
2 What would you do with the bath water after you have had a bath?
3 What do I do if a small piece of bread gets caught in my throat?
4 How did you get into your house when you found you had lost
your keys?
5 What did you do when you couldn't send the goods up to Scotland
by road?

6 Why do you draw the curtains in the front of your house?
7 What do you usually do when you hear a loud noise overhead?
8 If you arrived at a high-class restaurant dressed in very casual clothes, what might the manager do?

Particles expressing position or place

With certain verbs, for example, stative verbs (verbs that express a state), some particles are used with a positional sense. This means they express position, not movement. The main particles used in this way are
in, out up, down, on, back, away (= in another place)

a The main verbs are **to be, to stay, to stop, to remain, to leave, to keep, to hold**

I don't like flying. I'm always glad when *I'm down.*/ '*Is* John *in?*' 'No, I'm afraid *he's out.*/ Bill has been ill and he's not supposed to *be out* but I can't *keep* him *in.*/ I *keep* my hair *back* with a pin because it won't *stay back* by itself./ They forgot and *left* the flag *up* all night./ The deck of the bridge was *held up* by large cables./ The food was so bad that I could hardly *keep* it *down.*/ The boxer fell to the canvas and *stayed/remained down* for the count of ten./ You go ahead; I'll *stay back* and wait for the others./ I'm going on holiday — I'll *be away* for two weeks./ Come back soon — don't *stay away* so long this time./ 'Hold your hat on!' 'It won't *stay on*, the wind keeps blowing it off.'/ If you screw the top on hard, it will *stay/remain on*.

b to wait (only with **in** or **up**)

Come round to my place tonight. I'll *wait in* for you./ I've forgotten my key and I'll be late home tonight. Can you *wait up* for me?

c to lock, to shut (only with **in** and **out**)

Hold the door open, I don't want to be *locked in/out*.

d to find (only with **in** or **out**)

If you wish to see the principal you'll *find* him *in* at three o'clock.

Exercises

1 *Study the sentences below. In each space put either a suitable verb chosen from the ones discussed above or a suitable directional particle.*

1 We walked to the front door. I went to take my keys . . . . . . and found I had lost them. I must have . . . . . . them down somewhere in the restaurant. We were . . . . . . out.'

2 I watched the balloon rise . . . . . . above the trees. The balloon-ists' aim was to . . . . . . up for as long as possible. Unfortunately they were forced . . . . . . a few hours later by a severe electrical storm.

3 'If I call . . . . . . tonight will you . . . . . . in?' 'Yes, I will. I've been going . . . . . . too much lately and I've decided to . . . . . . in tonight and study.'

4 The roof of the old tunnel was . . . . . . up by large pieces of timber from which green slimy plants hung . . . . I looked . . . . . . over my shoulder but could see no light. The only thing to do was to keep moving . . . .

5 I went to Jane's place early this morning only to . . . . . . her out. Her mother said that she had gone . . . . . . for the day but would be . . . . . . at about 8 o'clock.

6 During the annual club meeting some of the members walked . . . . . . in protest. The chairman said, 'Now that they . . . . . . out, they can . . . . . . out.'

7 I'm . . . . . . away tomorrow and I'll probably . . . . . . away for a week. I'm flying . . . . . . to France and then I'm driving . . . . . . to the south of Spain.

8 Get . . . . . . the bus at this stop and . . . . . . on until you get to Oak Street. When you get . . . . . . make sure to . . . . . . your hat on or it will blow . . . . . . in this wind.

2 *Try to answer each of these questions using a phrasal verb with a positional particle chosen from those discussed above.*

1 When would you do if your husband came home at 4 o'clock in the morning?

2 What did you do when your husband wanted to fight with the drunken man in the restaurant?

3 What did the doctors do when they couldn't remove that piece of metal from Joe's back?
4 What are tent pegs used for?
5 What are the poles in a tent used for?
6 If you were expecting an old friend to come and visit you, would you go out?
7 Excuse me, but can I see the manager, Mr Jones?
8 What happens when a boxer receives a knock-out blow?

Off with verbs of motion and verbs implying motion

The use of **off** with these verbs can convey two ideas.

a the sense of going away, leaving for another place, or of causing something or someone to leave or go away.

to be, to carry, to clear, to drift, to drive, to fly, to gallop, to get, to go, to hurry, to make, to march, to pack, to ride, to run, to sail, to send, to sheer, to ship, to shoot, to take, to trot, to walk, to whisk

It's 8 o'clock, I'll *be off* now./ The injured man was *carried off* in an ambulance./ The policeman told the boys who were making a noise outside the old man's house to *clear off* (i.e. to go away quickly)./ Before the speaker had finished, the crowd began to *drift off* (i.e. go away slowly)./ He put the car in gear and *drove off* at great speed./ The blackbird alighted on a branch for a moment and then *flew off*./ The horse was frightened by the noise of the train and *galloped off*./ I must *get off* or I shall be late for work./ 'Has Bill gone?' 'Yes, he *went off* yesterday morning.'/ John said a few words to me then he *hurried off*./ The thief grabbed the woman's handbag and *made/ran/off*./ The soldiers *marched off* to war./ Your father said that if you don't behave, he'll *pack* you *off* to boarding school. She mounted her pony and *rode off*./ Columbus *sailed off* into the unknown./ It's Fiona's birthday on Thursday, I must *send* her present *off*./ I saw him coming towards me and waved but he *sheared off* and ran away in another direction./ Have the goods been *shipped off*?/ The plane *takes off* at 11 p.m./ Mary said something to Bill, turned, and *walked off*./ The little girl *wandered off* because she was bored. The Prime Minister arrived at the airport and was *whisked off* in an official car.

b **Off** can also convey a sense of *beginning* an action. Some verbs have both senses;

to be, to blast/lift (of rockets), **to lead/start, to set, to step**

In some sports **off** is used to indicate the beginning of a game or part of a game;

to kick (football), **to tee/drive** (golf), **to bully** (hockey)

When the horse race started the commentator shouted, 'They're *off!'*/ The expedition *takes off* from base camp next week./ I'll *start off* and you follow./ If we're going to climb the mountain we'll have to *set off* at dawn./ I don't know what *set* it *off* but there was a terrible argument at the meeting./ When the music begins *start off* with your left foot./ Thousands of people watched the rocket *blast/ lift off* for the moon./ 'When does the football match start?' 'Oh, they *kick off* at 3 p.m.' /The golfer said to his partner 'You *tee off* first.'

c Colloquial verbs that can be used with **off** are
to beetle, to buzz, to nip, to pop, to push, to shove, to slope, to swan

He dashed into the shop to buy a bottle and then *beetled off./* You're annoying me, *buzz/push/shove off./* I'll just *nip off* to the shops before lunch./ He looked rather suspicious, he hung around for a while and then *sloped off./* A cluster of photographers took pictures of the actress as she *swanned off.*

d The following verbs, although not verbs of motion, are verbs in which the particle expresses the initiative (i.e. the beginning) aspect of the verb;

to trigger, to spark, to touch
The Prime Minister's speech on taxation *triggered/sparked/touched off* a furious newspaper controversy.

e **See**, although not a verb of motion, is used with **off** to describe accompanying someone at the start of a journey.

I'll *see* you *off* at the airport.

Exercises

1 *Choose the correct verb from those given in brackets:*

  1 The old lady told the small boys who were stealing her apples to (walk/climb/clear/kick) off.

2 The boy stole an apple from the fruiterer's stall and (walked/made/whisked/went) off.

3 The yacht race is about to begin. Ah, there's the gun. They (sail/drift/clear/are) off now!

4 We have a long walk tomorrow. At what time do you think we should (set/walk/step/hurry) off?

5 The message boy jumped on his bicycle and (drove/rode/ran/got) off down the road.

2 *In each space below put* **either** *a suitable verb from those discussed above* **or** *a suitable particle. Discuss any alternatives.*

1 A few minutes after the teams had . . . . . . off there was a fight between two players.

2 No one knew what . . . . . . it off but the result was that one player was . . . . . . off by the referee.

3 The cowboy unhitched his horse, climbed . . . . . . and . . . . . . off without once looking . . . . . . A cloud of dust rose . . . . . . behind him.

4 The plane . . . . . . off at 6 a.m. tomorrow. To be on time you'll have to . . . . . . off from where you live at about 4 a.m. You can sleep after the plane . . . . . . off. The journey isn't long, so when you get . . . . . . in Paris you'll be feeling fairly fresh.

5 The speaker held out her hand . . . . . . and said to the crowd, 'Don't go . . . . . . , listen to me,' but they began to . . . . . . off one by one. Then she shouted, 'When I . . . . . . off I said I had an important message for you. If you want to hear it turn . . . . . . and come . . . . . . now.'

6 I have as much trouble . . . . . . my husband off to work as I do . . . . . . my children off to school. I always have to . . . . . . him off at the front door but even then he usually . . . . . . off without something important and has to come . . . . . . to get it. One day, I think, they'll come and . . . . . . me off to the madhouse.

7 Do you see that parcel on the top shelf? Will you get it . . . . . . please? I want to . . . . . . it off to Singapore today, and, if I don't . . . . . . it off this morning I'll miss the mail.

8 I . . . . . . off three applications for jobs last week but so far not one reply has come . . . . . . I think my letters must get sent . . . . . . into space somewhere.

9 The rocket . . . . . . off at 6 a.m. and thousands stood looking . . . . . . at it.

3 *Try to answer these questions using as many phrasal verbs as you can. Discuss any alternatives.*

1 Why couldn't you catch the pickpocket who stole your wallet?
2 What would you do if you saw a mad dog coming towards you?
3 How will you get to the airport on time to catch that early plane?
4 What might you say as an exciting motor race begins?
5 Why do you have to be at the airport at 7 a.m.?
6 What are you going to do with those job applications?
7 At what time does the football match begin tomorrow?
8 Can't you stay for a few minutes and have a cup of tea and a chat?
9 John and Jane are off to Australia tomorrow. What do you think we should do?
10 Why didn't any of the public have a chance to shake hands with the American president when he came out of No. 10 Downing Street?

4 *In each space in the sentences below put a suitable verb (not necessarily one of those already discussed) used with the particle* **off**.

1 When the sergeant gave the order the squad of soldiers . . . . . . to the sounds of drums and pipes.
2 The bird on the window sill . . . . . . when I made a sudden movement.
3 To begin this dance you must . . . . . . with your right foot.
4 When the sailor fired a shot into the water the shark that had been following the fishing boat . . . .
5 Listen. The dog is barking furiously outside. Something must have . . . . . . him . . . .
6 The demonstrators who were trying to force their way into the embassy compound . . . . . . when the police arrived.
7 There are many old stories about eagles which . . . . . . small children.
8 The player was having an argument with the referee but before the referee could . . . . . . him . . . . . . he turned and . . . . . . of his own accord.
9 The new space probe is due to . . . . . . at dawn tomorrow.
10 Fred . . . . . . on his round-the-world yacht trip tomorrow. I think I'll go and . . . . . . him . . . .

About and *around* with verbs of motion

When used with verbs of motion **about** and **around** convey the sense of movement without any pattern or aim to it — indiscriminate movement. They are usually interchangeable. Common verbs of motion used with these particles are:

a **to blow, to circle, to crowd, to gather, to go/to get, to dash, to drive, to float, to jump, to gallop, to move, to ride, to race, to reel, to stagger, to roll, to slip, to swim, to travel, to wander**

The girl's hair was *blown about/around* by the wind./ The hawk *circled about/around* above the meadow./ Katherine stays at home most of the time, she doesn't *get/go about/around* a great deal./ Whenever there is an accident people just seem to *crowd/gather about/around*./ I've been *dashing about/around* all morning trying to find a flat to rent./ Some people just get in their cars on a Sunday and *drive about/around*./ Bits of paper were *floating about/around* on the surface of the river./ The foals were *galloping about/around* in the field./ Young people like to *ride about/around* on their motor cycles./ Johnny, don't *race about/around* like that; you'll tire yourself out./ The drunken man was *reeling about/around* outside the pub./ Some of the ship's cargo had become loose and was *rolling about/around* on the deck./ Everyone was *slipping about/around* as the pavement was covered with ice./ I'll just dive in and *swim about/around* for a while./ The businessman said, 'I'm getting sick of all this *travelling about/around*, I must get a more settled job.'

b With some verbs, **about** and **(a)round** do have a definite directional sense — i.e. of turning in the opposite direction.

about face (military: American), **about turn** (military: British), **to**

come about (nautical), to face about, to go about (nautical), to spin about/(a)round, to turn about (a)round

Despite the helmsman's efforts the yacht would not *come about*./ When I tapped him on the shoulder he *faced/spun/about/around* and looked at me./ The water is too shallow here for the yacht; we'll have to *go about*./ We can't drive any further along this road — we'll have to *turn around/about* and go back.

Exercises

1 *In each space in the sentences below put* **either** *a suitable verb of motion* **or** *a suitable particle.*

1 When the old lady fell . . . . . in the street some people . . . . . around but no one offered to help her . . . . . Finally a young boy pushed his way . . . . . , held . . . . . his hand to the lady and tried to help her . . . . .

2 When the policeman stopped the man to ask him a question he immediately . . . . . around and ran . . . . . . The policeman set . . . . . after him but he got . . . . . in the crowd. The policeman . . . . . about in the area for a while but he didn't see him again.

3 The plane took . . . . . on time but when we got to our destination we had to . . . . . about for almost an hour before we could come . . . . . As we taxied . . . . . to the airport building we saw a lot of policemen . . . . . about and we realized that there had been some sort of emergency.

4 'When I went to see Joan this morning she wasn't . . . . . .' 'That's not surprising. She's often . . . . . . She . . . . . about quite a lot, you know.'

5 'Hello Marianne. This is a surprise. Come . . . . . .' 'Thanks. I'm glad I've found you . . . . . . When I set . . . . . from home I thought I knew where you lived but I've been . . . . . around for an hour trying to find the place. It's very windy outside and now my hair's all . . . . . about.

6 The small boy looked very tired. When the policeman went . . . . . to him he said he was lost. It seemed he had been . . . . . about for several hours. The kindly policeman picked him . . . . . and carried him . . . . . to the police station to phone . . . . . a report.

7 The patrol boat was just sailing . . . . . to base when the captain

received a message to . . . . . . about and look for a small boat
that was in trouble. When he reached the spot he found that the
boat had gone . . . . . . and there were several people . . . . . .
about in the water. They were picked . . . . . . frightened but
unhurt.

8 When the housewife phoned . . . . . . a report that she had seen
an escaped lion . . . . . . about in the park she triggered . . . . . .
a neighbourhood scare.

2 *In each of the sentences below choose the most suitable verb from
those given in brackets.*

1 Nomads are people who (walk/ride/wander/gallop) about from
place to place.
2 The garden was full of flowers among which dozens of butterflies
were (getting/gathering/dashing/flitting) about.
3 I'm tired out. I've been (dashing/circling/slipping/travelling) about
all morning trying to get some spare parts for our car.
4 The frail old man doesn't (jump/stagger/get/blow) about very much
but in fine weather he likes to (stroll/reel/race/turn) around the
park.
5 We haven't lived in the same house for more than two years on
end. My husband's job keeps up (driving/moving/rolling/slipping)
around.
6 The dead leaves were being (circled/floated/crowded/blown) about
by the strong wind.
7 When the man stood on a box in the park and began to speak, a
few people (gathered/circled/got/slipped) around.
8 In cowboy films we often see the vultures (circling/rolling/slipping/
crowding) about in the air above a dying man.

3 *Answer the following questions using as many phrasal verbs as you
can. Discuss any alternatives.*

1 What would you do if you were the skipper of a yacht and you
saw some dangerous rocks ahead?
2 What do people usually do when there is an accident?
3 What do you do when someone taps you on the shoulder and calls
your name?
4 When a man has drunk too much alcoholic liquor what does he do
when he tries to walk?
5 When little children are very excited what do they usually do?

28

6 When a person has recovered from a long illness what is one of the things he wants to do?
7 Why do people like to keep aquaria with tropical fish in them?
8 What do people often do when they can't get to sleep at night?

7 *About* and *around* with other verbs

The main use of these two particles is to convey the sense of a continuing action or state. There are other uses as you will see below. One is to convey a sense of lack of aim or purpose.

a to change, to feel, to fish, to gaze, to look, to order, to push, to shop, to spread, to stare, to swap, to switch
All these verbs imply motion or direction. The particle conveys the sense of 'here and there' or 'from place to place'. Some of them also have colloquial meanings.

My wife keeps *changing/swapping/switching* the living room furniture *around/about*./ He *felt/fished around/about* in his pocket for his bus fare./ On their first visit to London the children just *gazed/stared around/about*./ Because he was once an army officer he thinks he can *order* people *about*./ The little boy was happy *pushing* his toy car *about/around* for hours./ If you have any business at a government office, don't let those petty officials *push* you *around/about*. (= treat you carelessly or in a high-handed manner)/ You can buy clothes cheaply if you *shop around*./ There are always gossips who *spread* stories *around* concerning other people./ When I visited London my friend took me *about/around* in his car.

b to belt, to hit, to kick, to knock, to slap, to throw, to toss

When he got drunk he would go home and *belt/slap/knock* his wife *about/around*, so she left him./ I like to get on the tennis court and *hit/knock* the ball *around*./ The workers were *kicking* a ball *about/around* in the factory yard./ Because Keith has been made a prefect at school he thinks he can *kick* the other boys *about/around* (*fig.*). John has been in the army and has travelled to many parts of the world — he has *knocked about/around* quite a lot (*coll.*, = he has had a lot of different experiences)./ Don't *throw* your doll *about/around* like that; you'll break it./ When the bus stopped suddenly the passengers were *thrown/about/around*.

c to be, to keep, to hang, to stay, to stick, to wait
These verbs express a state rather than an action. The particles here has the sense of 'close at hand' or 'not far away.'

My mother is ill so I thought I'd better *be about/around* in case she needs me./ I won't be far away; I'll *hang/stick/stay around/about* for a while (*coll*)./ I always *keep* some money *about/around* in case I need it./ There are always a lot of people *waiting/hanging about* in railway stations.

d to come, to fiddle, to hang, to idle, to laze, to leave, to lie, to loaf, to mess, to potter, to sit, to stand
Most of these verbs also convey a state rather than an action. The particles usually convey a sense of purposelessness and often disapproval.

How did that *come about*? (= happen)/ My husband is always *fiddling/pottering/messing about/around* in his workshop./ I don't like to see all these young people *hanging/standing about* on street corners./ Too many young people today seem to spend their time just *idling/lazing/loafing about*./ When I go on holiday I just want to *laze about/around* in the sun./ Why do you *leave* all your school-books *around/about* for me to pick up?/ Who left these dirty shoes *lying about/around* all over the place?/ Young Joe is always *messing about/around* with that motor cycle of his./ I'm sick and tired of this insurance company — they keep *messing* me *about* (= dealing with me inefficiently). After a hard week's work at the office, I like to *potter around* and do odd jobs in the garden on Saturday./ Why don't you go and play tennis instead of just *sitting/standing around*?

e to clown, to fool, to horse, to monkey, to play
These convey the sense of acting in a foolish manner.

Some young lads were *clowning about/around* on their motor cycles when one fell off and broke his leg./ What on earth is that noise in the other room?' 'Oh it's only your two sons *horsing around/about*./ John, if you hadn't been *fooling/monkeying around/about*, you wouldn't have broken that window./ Sarah, settle down to do your homework and stop *playing around*.

f to bring, to go, to set

What *brought about* (= caused) the present state of affairs?/ I want to learn Russian but I'm not sure of how to *go/set about* (= start to do) it.

Exercises

1 *Choose the correct verb from those given in brackets.*

1 As it galloped by, the horse's long mane was being (tossed/thrown/ swapped/moved) about by the wind.
2 I wish my husband would mow the lawn on Sunday but all he wants to do is to (wait/stick/hang/loaf) about.
3 My wife always has to (move/push/fish/spread) around in her handbag whenever she wants some small change.
4 The small boys were (moving/pushing/taking/kicking) an empty jam tin around on the pavement.
5 I often go into big shops not to buy anything but just to (look/ switch/knock/push) around.
6 It is a good thing for young people to (knock/kick/spread/take) about a bit before they marry and settle down.
7 At their first sight of the Grand Canyon the tourists just stood and (waited/tossed/gazed/loafed) about.
8 'When can I see you again?' 'I don't know but I'm not going anywhere; I'll (keep/stand/sit/be) around.'

2 *In each space in the sentences below put **either** a suitable verb **or** a suitable particle. There may be alternatives. Discuss these.*

1 When I went to see the doctor he was . . . . . . on an urgent call and I had to . . . . . . about in his waiting room for about two hours.
2 The passenger was . . . . . . about in his pocket for his fare and the bus conductor said, 'I can't . . . . . . around here all day. If you haven't got the fare you'll have to get . . . .'
3 During the night one of the poles that held our tent . . . . . . broke and the whole thing fell . . . . . . Here we were . . . . . . about in the dark trying to find matches and candles. John didn't make himself very popular because he got angry and began to . . . . . . us around.
4 It was a lovely day and many people were . . . . . . about in the park arm in arm. The older people were . . . . . . about in the sun

on the park benches while the children played . . . . . . on the newly-cut grass.

5 Why do you want to . . . . . . around the house all day. Get . . . . . . and take some exercise. Phone one of your friends and . . . . . . him over then you can both go . . . . . . and . . . . . . a ball about somewhere. Anything's better than . . . . . . around like this.

6 Some people were . . . . . . about outside No. 10 Downing Street hoping to see the Prime Minister when she came . . . . . . They must have been . . . . . . around for an hour or more when the door opened and she came . . . . They caught no more than a glimpse of her because she was whisked . . . . . . in an official car. The people were disappointed and began to drift . . . .

7 Mary told me that Bill's wife had gone . . . . . . and left him. I told her that I didn't believe it. There are always people who start these stories . . . . . . and then others . . . . . . them around.

8 I thought I would . . . . . . around the other day for some clothes for my children. As I . . . . . . about from shop to shop I got angrier and angrier. It was the attitude of the shop assistants that set me . . . . Whenever I tried to attract their attention they seemed to be . . . . . . around vacantly. In some shops they took no notice of me at all but just . . . . . . about talking and joking. I'm afraid I'm not patient enough to . . . . . . about until some young assistant considers he has time to serve me.

3 *Answer each of these questions using as many phrasal verbs as you can.*

1 What do sheep and cows do in the fields?
2 What do you do when you can't find a small coin in your pocket?
3 If you get tired of the furniture arrangement in your bedroom what can you do?
4 If you want to find where you can buy the cheapest meat, what will you have to do?
5 What do people who work hard all the year like to do on holiday?
6 What do some people with a little authority often think they can do to the public?
7 What would you do for a foreign friend who came to visit your town for the first time?
8 What would you do if you came into the house and found a ceiling had fallen down?

4 *Choose the correct particle from those given in brackets.*

1 When we set (away/off/about/over) from home this morning the weather was fine. Now the rain is coming (down/on/in/past) in buckets.

2 The man was standing in the middle of the road waving his arms (around/up/out/away) so we stopped the car and got (off/down/out/away).

3 John and Mary said they'd be here by 8 o'clock. I'm not going to sit (around/in/down/on) any longer waiting for them. I have a headache and I'm going to lie (in/off/about/down).

4 I wouldn't like to be a football referee. From the time the teams kick (out/off/away/about) until the final whistle you have to race (across/up/down/about) like a madman. And then sometimes you have the unpleasant duty of sending a player (off/away/out/back).

5 The modern fear is that some fool will spark (off/away/up/around) a nuclear war and then the missiles will start flying (off/away/up/about) and raining (in/down/through/away) on all the major cities of the world.

6 'Oh, it's 8 o'clock. I have to get (out/away/through/around) now, I'm afraid.' 'I'll see you (out/away/past/through) then. Why don't you come (about/in/on/around) next week and we'll go (out/away/off/through) and see a film.' 'That's a good idea, but why don't you come (in/by/past/over) to my place at about 7 o'clock. I'll be waiting (on/through/about/in) for you."

7 'My wife's in the garden. She's always pottering (on/through/off/about) outside. I think she's putting (on/in/down/under) some plants. Just a minute and I'll call her (out/off/through/in).' 'Don't bother. I'll just sit (on/in/up/around) for a while until she comes.'

8 Nuclear weapons are not things to play (around/along/up/on) with. Once a missile has been sent (off/out/through/across) on its mission it just cannot be called (down/away/down/back).

5 *In each space below put* **either** *a suitable verb* **or** *a suitable particle.*

1 The boxer was getting badly . . . . . . about. It was obvious that his opponent was only . . . . . . about with him. Very soon he took a blow on the chin and went . . . . . . for the count of ten.

2 Some small birds came . . . . . . on the lawn and began to eat the crumbs that the girl had put . . . . . . for them. They hopped . . . . . . chirping merrily until the pet cat appeared and caused them to fly . . . .

3 When the pop group arrived at the airport the police had put
. . . . . . a barrier to keep the excited crowd . . . . Just as the
group appeared some young girls began to scream and this sparked
. . . . . . such a surge of excitement that the police thought it wiser
to whisk them . . . . . . in several cars. When they realised that
they had missed seeing their idols the disappointed crowd began
to drift . . . .

4 Not long after the yachts had got . . . . . . for the ocean race a
terrific storm swept . . . . . . suddenly from the north. The boats
were . . . . . . about helplessly in the angry seas. Some managed
to put . . . . . . and . . . . . . back to port but others unfortunately
went . . . . . . with their crews. A few days later a few shocked
survivors were found floating . . . . . . in rubber lifeboats.

5 After the film the other night I invited Bill . . . . . . for a few
drinks but I couldn't get him to go home. He kept hanging
. . . . . . talking and drinking until I was almost asleep. I hinted
that it was about time I got . . . . . . to bed but he took no notice.
In the end I almost had to . . . . . . him out. When I showed him
. . . . . . he had the cheek to say, 'Well, we must do that again
some time.'

6 The old lady who fell . . . . . . on the icy pavement was helped
. . . . . . by a policeman. He said in a kindly voice, 'Madam, this
is not the sort of weather for you to be . . . . . . in. It would be
wiser if you stayed . . . . . . until the weather improves'. The old
lady answered, 'Young man, the weather has never kept me
. . . . . . in the past and it won't in the future.'

6 *Answer each of these questions using as many phrasal verbs as you
can.*

1 What were the children doing in the park?
2 Helen had some bruises on her face. What happened to her?
3 What does your husband do in that workshop in the garage?
4 What happened at the airport last week when your flight was
delayed three hours?
5 How did young Philip break his arm?
6 What do some people in authority think they can do to other
people?
7 When some young people finish university, instead of settling down
and getting a job, what do they do?
8 What do some retired people like to do in their gardens?

Off expressing the completive sense of the verb

Off is used with certain common verbs to convey the sense of an action that is completed, is done thoroughly, or reaches some conclusion (or is to be completed, to be done thoroughly etc.).

a to bring, to carry, to pass, to pull
These verbs indicate success in doing something.

He has a scheme for making money but I don't think he can *bring/ pull* it *off*./ Everyone thought she would find making a public speech very difficult but she *carried* it *off* brilliantly./ The confidence trickster *passed himself off* (= successfully pretended to be) as a confidence trickster.

b to be

The meeting's *off* tonight (= cancelled)./ The party's *off* because Alexandra is ill./ I ordered soup but the waiter said that soup *was off* (= the restaurant had run out) so I had grapefruit instead.

c to doze, to drift, to drop, to snooze

These verbs can all be used instead of 'fall asleep'.

The television programmes are so bad that I *doze/drop/snooze off* every night./ Put the light out and he'll soon *drift off*.

d Other verbs with **off**

to beat, to buy, to call, to come, to cool, to die, to drink, to dry, to fight, to finish, to kill, to knock, to let, to pay, to polish, to show, to take, to write

At the end of two days the garrison had *beaten/fought off* the attack./ He threatened to expose me but I *bought* him *off* (= bribed him)./ The tennis match was *called off* (= cancelled)./ It's a good scheme but I don't think it will *come off* (= succeed)./ We went for a swim to *cool off*./ You're angry now but sit down for a while and you'll *cool off (fig.)*./ Most of the old people who knew the folk stories of this country have *died off*./ My roses have *died off* in the dry weather./ My roses have *died off* in the dry weather./ He picked up his glass of beer and *drank/tossed* it *off* without taking a breath (= drank it very quickly)./ After their swim they *dried off* in the sun./ That illness I had last year almost *finished* me *off*./ The dry weather has *killed off* the grass./ The tribe was *killed off* by the diseases introduced by the colonists./ You've been studying too hard; it's time you *knocked off* (= finished work)./ A leader of the underworld was *knocked off* (= murdered, *coll.*) last night by a rival organization./ They were supposed to deliver all the furniture but they *knocked off* (= stole, *coll.*) quite a few pieces./ The accused was *let off* with a warning./ I've closed the company and paid off all the staff./ I want to *pay off* the mortgage on my house before I'm fifty./ Study hard — it *pays off* (= is worth it)./ I can't eat this ice cream — *polish it off* (= finish eating it) for me./ Look at Sheila. She's showing off (= displaying) her new pearl necklace./ That child of Arabella's is always *showing off* (= behaving ostentatiously) in front of other people./ The car was so badly damaged that the insurance company *wrote it off* (= declared it worthless).

Exercises

1 *Choose the right particles from those in brackets:*

1 Jane called (about/through/round/past) last night to tell me that tonight's meeting is (about/down/away/off).
2 I must leave (away/down/out/off) being so careless; I lost another umbrella yesterday. I must have put it (down/in/on/at) somewhere and walked (past/over/around/off) without it.
3 The boxer danced (on/about/through/off) in the ring looking for a chance to polish his opponent (up/down/away/off). However his opponent was not so stupid as to stand (on/out/about/in) waiting to be knocked (off/down/through/in) and he managed to fight the other man (off/away/down/about) until the end of the fifteenth round.
4 When we set (away/about/over/off) from the house it looked like

rain as there were some black clouds floating (through/about/along/past) in the sky. However the clouds cleared (back/away/through/past) and we had a successful day at the beach.

5 The Parliamentary candidate walked (in/past/along/about) from house to house canvassing for votes. Although he had tried to win the seat before and failed, he thought that, with some luck, he might pull it (off/about/in/down) this time. As each householder opened the door and looked (away/down/past/out) he gave a little speech which he had learnt.

6 I've been running (over/away/around/down) on the tennis court all afternoon and I have to go (away/down/off/out) with Jane this evening. I wish I could call it (back/in/off/about) now as I feel so tired but I promised to take her to the new film that's showing. Anyway if it's boring enough I might be able to drop (down/in/off/around).

2 *Choose the correct verb from those given in brackets:*

1 He was very thirsty and he (topped/drank/pulled/tossed) off the glass of cold water.

2 The child was very tired and she (dozed/went/cooled/finished) off in her mother's arms.

3 All Fred's study and hard work has (left/pulled/finished/paid) off — he's now a director of the company.

4 Jane drove her car into a tree yesterday and it's been (carried/pulled/polished/written) off.

5 'Are you going to the committee meeting tonight?' 'No, it's been (left/knocked/called/set) off.'

6 This long spell of dry weather is making my flower plants (die/kill/polish/knock) off.

7 I think I'm getting a cold and I've been taking aspirins and drinking lemon drinks trying to (kill/knock/fight/carry) it off.

8 We were planning a holiday in Greece but I don't think it'll (come/pull/cap/bring) off now as my husband has to attend a conference.

9 We all lent John money for this scheme which, if it (brought/pulled/finished/came) off, would bring us a handsome profit but we've been waiting so long now that we may as well (set/leave/go/come) off hoping.

10 The champion said that he was going to win the tennis match but with the score at 2 all it was doubtful whether he would be able to (come/fight/pull/top) it off. However in the last set he easily (knocked/tossed/fought/finished) his opponent off: 6–0.

11 It's too hot to work in the garden. I think I'll (set/come/knock/ polish) off, go for a swim to (top/cool/swim/step) off and then (snooze/dry/clear/take) myself off in the sun.
12 When we (made/stepped/set/tent) off on our camping trip we were looking forward to a good holiday but it rained every day and the tent leaked.

3 *Answer each of these questions using as many phrasal verbs as you can.*

1 If you saw your friend working in his garden on a very hot afternoon in summer, what might you tell him and/or invite him to do?
2 What happened to all the tomato plants and lettuce plants in your garden?
3 After a small baby has been fed what does it usually do?
4 It snowed very heavily last Saturday. What happened to the football match?
5 Why did the boy who fell in the river with his clothes on sit in the sun for some time?
6 What did medieval people who lived in castles use boiling oil and heavy stones for?
7 What would you say to a friend who was hoping to complete an important business contract?

Up expressing the completive sense of the verb

The use of **up** to convey the sense of a completed action is probably the commonest use of a phrasal verb particle in English. It is easier to look at this use by dividing the verbs up into groups according to meaning.

Verbs of closing, enclosing, restricting

a to brick, to close, to dam, to lock, to seal, to shut, to wall

For safety reasons the entrance to the abandoned mine was *bricked/walled/sealed up*./ The Smiths are away and their house is *closed/shut up*./ Rivers in the mountains are *dammed up* to provide energy for electricity./ Our society *locks* criminals *up* in prison./

b to block, to choke, to clutter, to clog, to plug, to silt, to stop, to stuff

The street flooded because the drains were *blocked/choked/clogged up* with litter./ The students' room was *cluttered up* with books and sports equipment./ The boy's nose was bleeding and the doctor *plugged/stopped up* his nostrils with wads of cotton wool./ If the mouths of rivers become *silted up*, bad floods can result./ I have a bad cold and my nose is *stuffed up*.

c to bunch, to cage, to coop, to cram, to crush

It was hard to tell who was winning the race as the runners were so *bunched up*./ I do not like to see wild animals *caged up* in zoos./ Young people living in cities often have to live *cooped up* in small rooms and bedsitters./ The boy couldn't talk because he had *crammed* his mouth *up* with cake./ The passengers in the underground train were so *crushed up* that they could hardly move.

Verbs of fastening

d to belt, to buckle, to button, to chain, to fasten, to hook, to nail, to pin, to screw, to sew, to stitch, to tie, to tighten, to zip

Car drivers are advised to *belt* up before they drive off./ *Buckle* your shoes *up* properly, Josephine, or you will fall over./ Johnny, if you are going out, *button/fasten up* your coat./ That savage dog should be *chained/tied up*./ Will you *hook up* the back of my dress, please, Hilary?/ You can *nail* up those boxes now./ Could you *pin up* the hem of my new coat please, then I can *stitch* it *up*./ Put those screws in the engine cover and *screw/tighten* them *up*./ The government decided to *tighten up* (*fig.* = make stricter) the tax laws./ The pilot *zipped up* his flying jacket.

Verbs of packaging

e to box, to bundle, to crate, to pack, to parcel, to sew, to tie, to wrap

Those machines have to be *boxed/crated up* and shipped off to the Middle East./ I must *bundle up* those old clothes and send them to the refugees./ It was a cold day and the small girl was *bundled/wrapped* up in a large overcoat./ At the end of a holiday I hate having to *pack up* to go home./ 'Where's your car?' 'Oh it's *packed up* (*coll.*, = stopped functioning) and I don't think the garage mechanic can do anything about it this time./ It's 6 p.m., I think I'll *pack up* (*coll.*, = stop working) and go home./ Will you *parcel up* those purchases please and deliver them to my house?/ When he had stuffed the cushion, he *sewed up* the opening./ She *tied up* the neck of the sack and threw it in the river./ Well, now that the murderer has confessed, that just about *wraps/sews/ties* the case *up* (*coll.*, = finishes it satisfactorily).

Exercises

1 *In each space in the sentences below put a suitable verb from those discussed above, used with the particle* **up** *in the completive sense. Discuss any alternatives:*

1 If you are going out . . . . . . before you leave the house.
2 The windows of the empty house were . . . . . . to prevent squatters from getting in.
3 Many medieval seaports no longer exist because they have become . . . .

4 There was a hole in the petrol tank but I . . . . . . it . . . . . . with chewing gum.

5 Many people object to modern battery farming methods where animals are . . . . . . in tiny living areas.

6 The oil will not flow because the outlet pipe is . . . . . . with dirt.

7 Teenagers tend to . . . . . . their bedrooms with sports gear, records and pictures of pop stars.

8 The man had two deep cuts in his cheek and the doctor had to . . . . . . them . . . .

9 Put your warm coat on and . . . . . . it . . . . . . tightly because it's snowing outside.

10 I can't . . . . . . this belt. I'll have to make another extra hole in it.

11 When the central heating system was put in, the owner of the house . . . . . . all the open fireplaces as they were of no further use.

12 There is an old World War 1 song which says, '. . . . . . your troubles in your old kit bag and smile, smile, smile!'

13 'I see you've got a new motor bike. What happened to the old one?' 'Oh, it just . . . .'

14 I hate flying. I don't enjoy being . . . . . . with hundreds of other people in a flying sardine tin.

15 'Have you . . . . . . that business deal with the South Americans yet?'

2 *In each space put either a suitable verb from those discussed above or a suitable particle.*

1 Why do you leave all those old books lying . . . . . . ? Why don't you . . . . . . them up and send them . . . . . . to an auction?

2 Harbours at river mouths often become . . . . . . up because of the mud that is carried . . . . . . by flood waters.

3 If the mouth of that old well is not . . . . . . up, some child will . . . . . . in and kill itself.

4 If you're going . . . . . . this morning, ... yourself up well or you'll be half-frozen by the time you get . . . .

5 I can hardly breathe. I am all . . . . . . up with a cold. That's the result of being . . . . . . up in underground trains and waiting . . . . . . at cold bus stops.

6 If you don't . . . . . . up your house before you go . . . . . . you are likely to find that someone has broken . . . . . . while you have been . . . .

7 The children in this school fool . . . . . . too much — the discipline
   needs to be . . . . . . up.
8 'Those lions just seem to lie . . . . . . all day.' 'So would you if
   you were . . . . . . up like that.'
9 The student . . . . . up his bicycle so that no one could run
   . . . . . . with it.
10 The housewife said, 'I'm . . . . . . up with being . . . . . . up in this
   small house all day. I must go . . . . . . and get some fresh air.'

3 *Try to answer these questions using verbs with the particle* **up** *in the
completive sense and any other phrasal verbs.*

1 What is your teenage son's bedroom like?
2 What is it that you object to about zoos?
3 Why won't the water flow when I turn the tap on?
4 What am I going to do about this tear in my jacket?
5 What is it that you don't like about living in big cities?
6 The nuts holding the car wheel are loose. What shall I do?
7 How is water used to provide electrical energy?
8 What do you usually do with your Christmas presents?
9 What do you do if you are going out during very cold weather?
10 What do you do if your shoe-laces are undone?

10 *Up* expressing the completive sense of the verb: part 2

a Verbs of breaking, cutting, dividing

to bash, to break, to chop, to cut, to dig, to grind, to plough, to slice, to tear, to split

Bill hit a tree yesterday and *bashed* his car *up*./ The old ship was sold to be *broken up*./ If you're making stew, first *chop/cut* the meat *up* into small pieces./ Joan was very *cut/broken up* (= upset) about the failure of her marriage./ The farmer *dug up* some old Roman coins in one of his fields./ The newspaper reporter *dug up* (= found out) a lot of facts about the minister's resignation./ Wheat is *ground up* to make flour./ They *ploughed up* the lawn so that they could grow more potatoes in the ground./ The thieves *split up* the money between them./ They were once partners but they have *split up* (= left each other) now./ Angrily she *tore up* his letter.

b Verbs of gathering, collecting

to gather, to gang, to heap, to pile, to rake, to round

The lecturer *gathered up* her notes and left the room./ After the football match some supporters *ganged up* and roamed around the streets./ A lot of small boys *ganged up* on the school bully and gave him a beating./ *Heap up* those leaves and we'll burn them./ *Pile* those boxes *up* in the corner please./ The money in the bank is *piling up* (*fig.*). Every autumn I *rake up* the fallen leaves./ I can't even *rake up* (= get together with difficulty) enough money for a holiday this year./ *Round up* a few people and we'll have a game of football.

c Verbs of cleaning etc.

to brush, to clean, to mop, to rub, to scrape, to scrub, to swab, to sweep, to tidy, to wash, to wipe

My old hat looks quite new now I've *brushed* it *up*./ I must *brush up* (= revise) my French before my holiday in Paris./ Mary, *clean up* that mess you've made!/ Sebastian left the bath tap running and flooded half the house. We've been hours *mopping/swabbing* it *up*./ Once I've *rubbed* that old brass vase *up* it'll look like new./ There's mud on the floor; *scrape* it *up* please./ Before surgeons perform an operation they always *scrub up*./ The carpenter *swept up* the sawdust underneath the bench./ Just a moment, I'll go and *tidy* myself *up*./ I hate *washing up* (i.e. the dishes) after a meal./ George used to be a good boxer but he's *washed up* (= no longer any good) now./ Please *wipe up* that coffee you spilt.

d Verbs of dressing

to make, to dress, to smarten, to tog

My wife takes hours to *make* herself *up*./ The little boy was all *dressed up* for the party./ My sister *dresses* herself *up* on Saturday to go to the disco./ Hello Edward, why have you *smartened* yourself *up* today?/

e Verbs of causing confusion

to botch, to bungle, to foul, to mess, to muck, to screw

All of these are colloquial.

The travel agent has *botched/bungled/messed/mucked* up our holiday arrangements./ The athletics meeting was *fouled up* by bad weather./ John's a fool. I gave him simple instructions and he *screwed* them *up* (a very strong term — only to be used to people you know well).

f Verbs of ceasing or refusing to talk

to shut, to belt, to button, to clam

These are all colloquial.

I'm sick of listening to your whining. Why don't you *belt/shut/button up*?/ The police tried to question the suspect but he *clammed up* (= refused to talk).

g Verbs of eating, feeding

to chew, to drink, to feed, to fatten, to eat, to gobble, to swallow;

Chew up your food before you swallow it./ *Drink up* your milk./ *Eat up* your vegetables./ John looks thin after his illness. He needs *feeding up*:/ We are *fattening up* that turkey for Christmas dinner. Eat properly Bill, don't *gobble* your food *up* like that./ During the earthquake the ground opened and *swallowed up* several houses.

h Verbs of measuring, calculating

To add, to count, to even, to measure, to reckon, to settle, to tot

Will you *add/tot up* that list of figures please. The detective was puzzled. All the information about the case didn't *add up* (= make sense). When the shopkeeper *counted/reckoned up* at the end of the sale he found he had made a good profit./ If I'm going to wallpaper this room, I'll have to *measure it up* first./ John's so young to be in the army.' 'Don't worry; he'll *measure up* (= come up to standard).'/ John, you owe me £10.00. Now's the time to settle up./ We have two cars so, if four people go in each, that will *even* things *up*.

i Verbs of confusing

to jumble, to mix, to muddle

I took the car engine to pieces, then I managed to *jumble/mix* the parts *up* and I had difficulty getting it back together again./ When I try to do simultaneous equations in algebra I always get *muddled up*.

j Verbs of injuring (all colloquial)

to beat, to bash, to rough.

The member of the gang who gave information to the police was badly *beaten/bashed up* by unknown assailants./ The film star who didn't like his photograph being taken grabbed the camera and *roughed up* the camera man.

k Verbs of preserving, saving

to save, to store, to treasure

Bill and Mary have *saved up* enough money to buy a house./ Animals that hibernate *store up* food in their body tissues./ As we get older we tend to *treasure up* memories of our youth.

l Verbs connected with cold weather

to freeze, to frost, to ice, to snow

It's early autumn now but in a few months everything will be *frozen up*./ The windscreen of my car was *frosted up* this morning./ Refrigerators will not work properly if they get *iced up*./ The weather report said that all the roads in the north were *snowed up up*.

Exercises

1 *Choose the appropriate verb from those given in brackets.*

1 George says his marriage is a mess. He and his wife are considering (piling/messing/wrapping/splitting) up.
2 The rider was killed when his motor bike (crushed/piled/heaped/broke) up against a tree.
3 He wrote a lot of good books in his youth but as a writer he's now (torn/wiped/washcd/shut) up.
4 Let's (round/gang/sweep/heap) up a few friends tonight and have a party.
5 The archaeological party (swept/ploughed/dug/raked) up evidence of a previously unknown civilization.
6 The evidence of the accused's guilt was slowly (gathering/heaping/rounding/piling) up.
7 Some of the children volunteered to stay after school and (brush/paint/sweep/wash) up the classroom.
8 Joan was very rude to me. I was giving her some advice and she told me to (close/tighten/belt/buckle) up.
9 Don't let Bill make the arrangements for the picnic as he'll only (mess/wipe/bundle/pile) them up again.
10 It takes a long time for an actress to (scrub/tidy/tog/make) herself up before going on stage.

2 *Complete each of the sentences overleaf by using a suitable verb with the particle* **up** *in the completive sense. Discuss any alternatives.*

1 After the outdoor music festival the workers had to . . . . . . up the site. All the litter was . . . . . . up and then . . . . . . up ready to be burnt. The ground too had to be levelled off because it had been . . . . . . up.

2 The new police chief decided to . . . . . . the town up and the first thing he did was to . . . . . . up a lot of known petty criminals.

3 What is Barbara so . . . . . . up about?' 'Oh, she feels that her marriage is . . . . . . up.'

4 Oh, now I've . . . . . . up my lipstick. Why do you keep talking to me while I'm . . . . . . myself up?

5 Help me . . . . . . up this kitchen, will you? The floor is filthy so you can . . . . . . up while I . . . . . . up this mess of dishes in the sink.

6 It's no wonder he didn't get the job, he looks such a mess. He ought to . . . . . . himself up a bit.

7 Did you get any information out of that suspect? Nothing at all. Someone . . . . . . up the interrogation and only succeeded in making him . . . . . . up.'

8 I'm afraid I can't . . . . . . up enough enthusiasm to go to the lecture. Once that speaker starts he never knows when to . . . . . . up.

9 I see you're all . . . . . . up for your job interview. Well, take care not to . . . . . . it up as you did last time.

10 After a lot of asking around the newspaper reporter managed to . . . . . . up a lot of information about the murder but many of those interviewed quickly . . . . . . up when they knew what he was doing.

3 *Try to answer these questions and complete these conversations using verbs with the particle* **up** *in the completive sense and any other phrasal verbs. Work in pairs.*

1 Your garden is in a mess. This is what you should do. You should . . .

2 All right Joan, so you're going to help me give the house a thorough cleaning. Well these are the things I want you to do. First . . .

4 What happened to the arrangements for the annual dance?

5 Where did the museum get those ancient coins and vases from?

6 'Why isn't Edith driving her car this week?' 'Oh didn't you hear, she . . .'

7 I heard that the office boy was rude to the manager. What did he say to him?

8 'Does your little daughter like going to parties?' 'Oh yes, she loves to . . .'

9 'What's wrong with Edith lately? Is there something the matter with her marriage?'

10 'Can you afford to go on holiday this year?' 'Yes, I think I can . . .'

4 *Choose an appropriate verb from those given in brackets:*

1 John doesn't seem to think clearly. His ideas are very (mixed/ botched/cluttered/cut/heaped) up.

2 In winter sometimes the water in the car radiator (blocks/chokes/ snows/messes/freezes) up.

3 The barman in the hotel was badly (mixed/torn/roughed/rubbed/ piled) up when some drunken football supporters (gathered/ ganged/piled/belted/heaped) up on him.

4 The deposit we paid to buy this house has (raked/sliced/fed/mud- dled/swallowed) up all our savings.

5 If you want to go on a holiday this year you had better start (saving/storing/raking/heaping/rounding) up now.

6 Five prisoners broke out from the prison last night but the police soon (raked/piled/rounded/gathered/bundled) them up.

7 NONDOL — this word contains letters which spell the name of a city but they are (jumbled/messed/piled/heaped/chopped) up.

8 We've agreed to (mix/add/tear/split/chop) up the cost of the meal between us but I'll pay the bill now and we can (tot/add/save/close/ settle) up later.

9 I have just been (reckoning/piling/gathering/settling/rounding) up the cost of redecorating the house. I've got all the figures, now I'll just (even/measure/save/gather/tot) them up.

10 The young man said, 'If you give me the job, I'll do my best sir. I am sure I can (even/fatten/gang/measure/make) up to it.'

5 *In each space in the sentences below put any suitable verb with the particle* **up** *in the completive sense. Discuss any alternatives.*

1 Look, it's all white outside. The garden is . . . . . . up. If you're going out . . . . . . yourself up well.

2 The old family photographs my grandmother had . . . . . . up for years are now quite valuable.

3 The instructions that come with some of these 'do-it-yourself' materials . . . . . . me up rather than help me.
4 'Billy, if you don't . . . . . . up your vegetables you can't have any sweets.'
5 The boy was . . . . . . up on his way own home from school by a group of older boys who . . . . . . up on him.
6 Two boys were lost in the cave for two days. When they had been found, the authorities decided to . . . . . . the entrance.
7 The union organizer said, 'Well I think that our deal with the management is just about . . . . . . up now.'
8 The modern world is a confusing place. It's no wonder so many young people get so . . . . . . up.
9 During the bad winter everything in the South of England . . . . . . up for several weeks. When the damage was . . . . . . up it came to millions of pounds.
10 The police had several theories about the series of unsolved bank robberies but they didn't seem to . . . . . . up.

6 *In each space in the sentences below put an appropriate particle.*

1 When we set . . . . . . from London our plan was to drive . . . . . . to Scotland. After some time, however, we heard over the car radio that all the roads in the north were frozen . . . . . . so we turned . . . . . . and drove . . . . . . to London.
2 Someone has messed . . . . . . my hi-fi set by playing . . . . . . with it and what is more, all my records are jumbled . . . .
3 After a policeman had been beaten . . . . . . in a lonely street a number of suspects were rounded . . . . . . by police cars. However, when those responsible were found the police called . . . . . . this operation.
4 The cattle were wandering . . . . . . over a large area and it was the cowboys' job to round them . . . . . . and drive them . . . . . . to a central place.
5 'Where's Jean? Is she . . . . . . ?' 'Yes, she's upstairs smartening herself . . . . . . to go . . . . . . with Bill.' 'You can go . . . . . . if you want to. You'll find her in front of the mirror making herself . . . .'
6 The water won't drain . . . . . . of the sink. I suppose it's blocked . . . . . . with tea leaves and food scraps. We'll have to use a plunger to force the blockage . . . . When you wash . . . . . . will you please be careful and don't choke the pipe . . . . . . again.

7 The work has been piling . . . . . . at the office. I didn't knock
. . . . . . until 9 o'clock last night. I wish I could get . . . . . . for
a few weeks' holiday, but that's impossible. If I went . . . . . . at
this time it would mess . . . . . . the whole routine of the office.

8 'I'm . . . . . . to Paris for a holiday next week'
'What day are you going . . . . . . ?'
'I'm going . . . . . . on Monday and coming . . . . . . on Friday.'
'Well, you had better brush . . . . . . your French before you go.'

7 *Try to answer these questions and complete these conversations using
verbs with the particle* **up** *in the completive sense and any other phrasal
verbs. Work in pairs.*

1 What is it you dislike about the winter most of all?
2 If young married couples want to buy a house, what do they have
to do?
3 If you are keeping some turkeys or geese for Christmas dinner,
what do you do with them?
4 We are going to redecorate this room with new wallpaper, carpets
and so on. Now this is what I want you to do. First of all . . .
5 What do young puppies and playful dogs sometimes do to slippers
if you leave them lying about on the floor?
6 What happens to refrigerators if you don't defrost them regularly?

Other common verbs used with *up*

a The following verbs are also used with **up** in the completive sense. They are, however, more difficult to group according to meaning.

to act, to play This can mean either to act in such a way as to draw the attention and disapproval of others, or to cause trouble.

Johnny, if you *act/play up* at the doctor's I won't buy you any sweets./ I can't play tennis today — my rheumatism is *acting/playing up*.

to back
If you ask the boss for more wages, we'll *back* you *up* (= support).

to be

It's 9 o'clock. *Isn't* George *up* (= out of bed) yet? The examination supervisor said 'Stop writing. Time's *up* now.' (= set period of time is completed)/ The prisoner's sentence *is up* tomorrow — he can go free./ When my car hit that tree at 70 mph I thought *it was* all *up* with me (= I was about to die)./ 'What's *up* with Jane? (= what's the matter with her?) She didn't speak to me this morning.

to blow This can mean to destroy with explosives or to inflate.

The old bridge was *blown up* because it was too dangerous./ The children were *blowing up* balloons for the party.

to bolster

Her husband was very insecure so she was always having to *bolster* him *up* (= reassure and support him).

to bottle

Bill was terrified of dogs but he never mentioned it. He kept it *bottled up* (= suppressed his emotions).

to build

What he did was a piece of youthful foolishness. There's no need to *build* it *up* into a criminal act.

to buy

Some commercial interests tried to *buy up* all the copper available on the world's markets.

to check

'What time does the plane take off?' 'Don't worry, I'll *check up* for you.' (= make sure of the facts)/ You had better get to work on time tomorrow. They're *checking up* on us (= investigating).

to do

The young couple bought an old house and *did* it *up*. (= renovated it)/ I feel *done up* (= exhausted) after a day at the office.

to be fed

I'm *fed up* with this job; I need a change./ I'm *fed up* with you and your complaints; I'm not going to listen any more.

to hush

The fact that a member of the royal family was the cause of a car accident was *hushed up* (= kept secret).

to live (it)

The bank robber was caught *living it up* (= living extravagantly) in the south of France.

to loosen

I do a few exercises every morning just to *loosen up* (= relax)./ Barbara is a very formal person; I wish she'd *loosen up* a bit./ They have *loosened up* (= made less strict) the laws about gambling.

to make

We need £1000 to *make up* the sum for building the old people's home./ Joan built some material for new curtains but she hasn't *made* them *up* yet (= completed them)./ John is very good at *making up* (= fabricating) excuses for not doing any work./ I can't *make up* my mind where to go for my holiday./ My parents helped me complete my studies but I'll *make* it *up* (= repay) to them one day.

to open

This room is stuffy; let's *open* it *up* and get some fresh air./ The USA was *opened up* by great railway networks./ When he was on a deserted stretch of motorway Bill *opened up* (= accelerated fully) his new sports car.

to finish, to end

The children started off by playing nicely together, but they *finished/ ended up* by fighting.

to follow

The police caught the murder by *following up* a few small clues./ The boss was pleased with my work last week. I think I'll *follow* that *up* and ask for a rise.

to give

In Dickens' *Tale of Two Cities* Sydney Carton *gave up* his life for a friend and died on the guillotine./ The escaped prisoner *gave* himself *up* to the police./ The climber *gave up* his attempt to reach the summit of the mountain and came back down./ I have decided to *give up* (= stop) smoking. He is so ill that the doctors have *given him up* (= lost hope for him)./ The crew of the ship that sank in the hurricane were *given up* for lost.

to grow

What are you going to be when you *grow up*, Andrew?

to hurry

Hurry up or we'll miss the train.

to own (= to confess)

Jean *owned up* to having spread stories about Mary's marriage./ He *owned up* to the theft.

to pull (= to stop)

A driver must *pull up* at red lights./ The rider *pulled* his horse *up* suddenly.

to put

Where did you *put up* (= stay) when you were in London?/ If you come to London we can *put* you *up* (= accommodate).

If **with** is added to the phrasal verb, the meaning changes to *tolerate*.

I can't *put up* with stupidity./ The teacher said 'I won't *put up* with this careless work any longer.'

to pay

You owe me £10.00. Come on now, *pay up*.

to sell (= to sell everything)

The Smiths have *sold up* and gone to Australia.

to set

The government *set up* an enquiry into the riot./ The newly-married couple *set up* house in London./ When he had finished his studies, Richard's father *set* him *up* (= provided sufficient money for) in business.

to sum up (= to summarize)

At the end of the trial the judge took over an hour to *sum up*./ At the end of his lecture the speaker said 'Now let me *sum up* briefly'.

to take

I like golf but it *takes up* too much of my time./ The fat man was *taking up* the whole seat./ I might *take up* (= accept) your offer of accommodation in London some weekend./ The young musician was *taken up* by the famous pianist (i.e. he became her protégé)./ Henry got into trouble with the police when he *took up* (= associated) with some bad companions.

to turn, to show

Bill *turned up* an hour late last night./ Hundreds of people *turned/ showed up* at the meeting.

to wake

Come on, *wake up*. It's 8 o'clock./ I wish the City Council would *wake* itself *up* (*fig.* — be more energetic) and get something done about the place./ Jack, if you want to get on in the business world you must *wake* your ideas *up* (*fig*).

to wind

The clock has run down; *wind* it *up* please./ After the cinema last night a group of us *wound up* (= ended up) at a night club./ Take those wet clothes off or you'll *wind up* with a bad cold./ The athlete said he was always *wound up* (= in a state of high nervous tension) just before a race.

to write

The mayor was involved in a minor car accident and it was *written up* in the local newspaper.

Other uses of *up*

b **to bring, to come, to crop, to get (to), to hold, to lay, to let, to pick, to speak, to take, to touch, to work**

Bill will *bring* that matter *up* (= introduce) at the meeting. We all try to *bring* our children *up* (= rear) properly./ Sorry I'm late but something *came/cropped up* (= happened suddenly)./ When children are left alone you never know what they *get up* to./ I'm late; I was *held up* (delayed) by the traffic./ Armed robbers *held up* the bank today and got away with £50 000./ Susan has broken her ankle and will be *laid up* for at least a week./ You are working too hard. Why don't you let up? (= go more slowly)./ Julie *picked up* quite a lot of French when she was in Paris./ Everyone was criticizing Jill but Pat *spoke up* (= gave her opinion courageously) for her./ Stephanie has decided to *take up* karate./ The paintwork in that corner looks a bit patchy, I'll *touch* it *up* tomorrow./ I can't really *work up* much enthusiasm for this party.

Exercises

1 *In each space in the sentences below put an appropriate verb with the particle* **up** *in the completive sense:*

1 That chest trouble of yours seems to be . . . . . . up again. Isn't it about time you . . . . . up smoking?
2 It's December 1 today; the year . . . . . . almost up. You had better . . . . . . up if you want to get your Christmas cards sent off in time.
3 Will you . . . . . . up on whether Mr Smith wants to sell his shares in the company? If he does, we'll . . . . . . them up.

56

4 We were . . . . . up with living in a small flat in the city. Then the chance of buying this old house in the country . . . . . up. So we did buy it and . . . . . it up.
5 If you don't . . . . . up your habit of being rude to the boss, you're going to . . . . . up by being out of a job.
6 I . . . . . up. I just haven't got enough breath in me to . . . . . up all these balloons.
7 Henry was a quiet little man who seemed to . . . . . up all his feelings inside him but his wife always . . . . . him up as though he were a forceful and decisive person.
8 'Why did you buy Jean that chemistry set. She'll . . . . . herself up.' 'Oh, do be sensible. She's no longer a child; she's . . . . . up you know.'
9 The union organizer . . . . . up by giving a summary of the workers' demands and those present at the meeting said that they would . . . . . him up in any action he took.
10 You must make a habit in life of . . . . . up even the smallest advantage and, if you do that, you'll . . . . . up a successful man.

2 *In each space in the sentences below put either an appropriate particle, or an appropriate verb. Discuss any alternatives:*

1 This cold weather has spoilt my garden. The plants were just . . . . . up when this cold spell killed them . . . . . . But I won't . . . . . up; I'll just . . . . . some more in next week.
2 I was just sitting . . . . . in the garden enjoying the sunshine when my wife hurried . . . . . and said, 'Hurry . . . . . and go and tidy yourself: 'Don't you remember that you asked the Smiths . . . . . for a few drinks. They'll be here any minute now.'
3 I'm afraid Jim has messed . . . . . the arrangements for the staff Christmas party. When we started . . . . . we had great ideas but it looks as though the whole thing will end . . . . . as a mess. I can't . . . . . up the energy to do anything about it.
4 When Jean was small she said that when she . . . . . up she was going to be a famous actress. She always spoke about how good she was but everyone thought she was merely . . . . . herself up. But she did have talent and also she started . . . . . with this strong determination to succeed. She never . . . . . up now and she has just about ended . . . . . where she said she would.
5 The old factory chimney was about to fall . . . . . and so it was decided to . . . . . it up. When the explosives were finally set . . . . . the whole structure came . . . . . in a cloud of dust.

6 'Why don't you . . . . . up the house? The place is cluttered
. . . . . with toys and all sorts of junk. Just look at the stuff that's
lying . . . . . on the table. I don't know what's . . . . . with you
lately. I can't stand it any longer. I'm . . . . . out.'
'Well when you come . . . . . you won't find me . . . . . because
I'm going . . . . . too. It's no fun being . . . . . up in this small
place all day.'
7 Mr. Smith is driving . . . . . to London tomorrow. There are a
few details that have to be tied . . . . . in connection with that
Arabian contract. I must say that at one stage I didn't think it
would . . . . . off as everything seemed to be so mixed . . . . . .
However, Smith refused to . . . . . up and now all that remains
to be done is to sign it.
8 'I'm . . . . . up with this job and this place. I think I'll pack
. . . . . and go . . . . . somewhere else. I've got a little money
. . . . . up so I may as well go . . . . . to Europe.'
'If I could . . . . . up enough money just now I'd come with
you.'

3 *Try to answer these questions and complete these conversations using
verbs with the particle,* **up** *in the completive sense, and any other
phrasal verbs. Work in pairs.*

1 How would you tell a young boy or girl to keep trying in life so
that they will finally become a success?
2 The room that you live in is not very tidy or attractive. Tell your
room-mate what you think ought to be done with it to improve it.
3 Imagine you have a child and he is going out to play in the snow
in very cold weather. Give him some instructions about how to
dress and what to do before going out.
4 'Jean, I want to post these books to India. Would you mind
. . .?'
5 Someone is annoying you and you don't feel like being very polite
to him. How can you tell him to keep quiet and go away?
6 There are some old mine buildings and dangerous mine shafts in
your area. What do you think should be done to them for the sake
of safety?
7 How do some girls like to get themselves ready when they are
going out to a party?
8 What might a radio news reader say to announce that there was
no hope of finding any crew members from the wrecked ship?

4 *Complete each of the following sentences by using the particle* **up** *with one of the verbs discussed above.*

1 If you take too much interest in the affairs of the club, you'll . . . . . by being on the committee and you'll find that that will . . . . . . a great deal of your time.
2 Betty was very kind to me. I . . . . . . her offer of a £1000 loan to start my business but some day I'll . . . . . . to her.
3 When Mary first . . . . . her business she was full of enthusiasm but in a few years she was bankrupt and had to . . . .
4 The story of the firm's important director who got away with thousands of pounds and who was found . . . . . . in South America was . . . . . . by the company because they didn't want a scandal.
5 I have a serious decision to make which will affect my whole future. I've got to . . . . . . my mind today but in a situation like this I get so . . . . . that I find it difficult to think.
6 It's about time the local town council . . . . . . up their ideas. Look at all that waste land on the edge of the town, for instance. Why don't they . . . . . . that . . . . . for development?
7 Being a businessman I play golf every week-end because I find it . . . . . . me . . . . . . If I didn't do that, I would probably . . . . . . with a nervous break-down.
8 The clerk took £5.00 from the petty cash with the intention of . . . . . . it . . . . . . later but when the loss was discovered he decided to . . . . . and take the consequences.
9 The defendant, who had failed to . . . . . . at a red light, ... a wonderful story about some peculiarity of his eyesight, but the magistrate fined him £50.00 and he had to . . . . . . or go to gaol.
10 When the court case was . . . . . . in the newspapers most commentators admitted that before the jury retired to consider the verdict the judge had . . . . . . in a masterly way.

5 *In each space in the sentences below put one of the following particles:* **off, up, about/around**

1 When I walked . . . . . . to him and tapped him on the shoulder he spun . . . . . . with a surprised look on his face.
2 John, you're overworking, overeating, and overdrinking. If you're not careful all this will finish you . . . . . . and you'll end . . . . . . under a tombstone.

3 Whenever I sit . . . . . . in the house with nothing to do I usually finish . . . . . by dropping . . . . Then, when I wake . . . . . . I feel dull and irritable.

4 The parliamentary candidate managed to rake . . . . . . a few supporters at his meeting but in the first half hour most of them had drifted . . . . When, after more than an hour's talking he said, 'Now to sum . . . . . . ,' there were only two people left in the hall. At his next meeting fewer people still turned . . . . . . The trouble is that people can't put . . . . . . with his boring manner of talking.'

5 We went to the airport to see our friends . . . . . . to America but we missed them in the crowd and after hanging . . . . . . for an hour or so we got fed . . . . . . and came home.

6 If you're going to walk . . . . . . outside in this freezing weather you had better wrap yourself . . . . . . well, otherwise you're going to wind . . . . . with a case of frostbite.

7 I think that Joe is washed . . . . . . as a boxer. Did you notice how clumsily he shuffled . . . . . . during his last bout and every time he was knocked down he took at least seven counts to get . . . .

8 All we have to do now is to parcel . . . . . . those books so that they can be mailed . . . . . . tomorrow morning. Well, don't just stand . . . . Wake . . . . . . and get it finished and then we can knock . . . . . . for the day.

6 *Choose the correct verb from those given in brackets.*

1 That car of mine is (doing/acting/finishing/messing/loosening) up again. I'm afraid that it's about to (end/wind/pack/botch/foul) up.

2 The little girl liked to (paint/make/wrap/button/dress) up in her mother's clothes and she also liked to (do/tog/tidy/clean/make) herself up with lipstick and powder.

3 Barbara was extremely (split/cut/ground/sliced/bashed) up when her marriage with Jim (acted/gave/broke/did/messed) up.

4 It was closing time at the pub and the landlord had just said, '(drink/end/swallow/settle/pile) up gentlemen; it's time to go home,' when a drunken voice said, 'Oh, (close/clam/wrap/buckle/belt) up!'

5 'The way you drive you're a danger to the public. You should be (chained/locked/closed/caged/cooped) up. Anyway I'm certain that that's how you'll (settle/sum/grow/gather/wind) up — in a police cell.'

60

6 Although the City Council tried to (stop/hush/bottle/clam/close) up the financial scandal, the story was leaked to the newspapers and (painted/opened/followed/summed/written) up on the front pages.

7 At any small disappointment George is liable to (stop/finish/feed/cut/give) up. I think he needs a little bit of (bashing/making/bolstering/measuring) up as he lacks confidence.

8 'How did your car get all (bashed/roughed/mixed/ground/muddled) up like that?' 'Oh, I lent it to a friend and he (screwed/piled/gathered/ground/crammed) it up on the motorway.'

9 'Why are you driving so slowly in such a powerful car? Come on, (take/wake/wind/loosen/open) her up.' 'Not on your life. There's a speed limit here and I don't want to (sum/wind/follow/settle/stop) up in court.'

10 You've been looking so (clammed/fattened/fed/choked/shut) up lately, Edith. What's the matter? You can tell me. It's no use (bottling/cooping/caging/wrapping/tieing) things up. They only (grow/build/tighten/close/round) up and get worse in the end.'

7 *Try to answer these questions and complete these conversations using verbs with the particle* **up** *in the completive sense and any other phrasal verbs. Work in pairs.*

1 What would you do if you won £500 000 on the football pools?
2 Why do you do those exercises so early in the morning?
3 What usually happens if you have a business such as a men's clothing shop, and you go bankrupt?
4 It's nearly 9 a.m. and Jane's still asleep upstairs; so this is what I want you to do. Go . . . .'
5 'Old Uncle Jim used to tell the most wonderful stories about his adventures in Africa. Do you think they were true?'
'No, I think . . . .'
6 How do you feel before a very important examination?
7 What do most people try to do if something has happened in their family that they don't want other people to know about?
8 What is really the best thing to do if you have done something wrong and you know that you will be discovered sooner or later?
9 What would you do if someone bet you that you couldn't translate a letter into English for him?
10 What do you do about accommodation when you go over to France in the summer?

12 The use of the particle *down*

The particle used to express completion of an action

a In this sense down is commonly used with verbs of securing. The main verbs used in this way are:

to batten, to clamp, to glue, to gum, to hammer, to hold, to nail, to peg, to pin, to paste, to staple, to stick, to strap, to tack, to tie

When the hatches are put over the hold of a ship they are then *battened down*./ He closed the lid of the trunk and *clamped* it *down*./ The tax authorities decided to *clamp down* on (= take firm measures to stop) tax evaders. Put those papers in that large envelope and *glue/gum/paste/stick* the flap *down*./ When you've put the lid on that crate *hammer/nail* it *down*. The wrestler *held* his opponent *down*./ George *holds down* a very responsible job in a government department (i.e. he is capable of doing it). If you don't *peg* your tent *down* properly it will blow away in a wind./ Before beginning to draw the diagram he *pinned* the paper *down* with drawing pins./ It is difficult to *pin down* (= define) the meaning of the word 'democracy'. The patrol was *pinned down* (unable to move) on the hillside for two days by enemy fire./ Joan is always changing her mind; you can't *pin* her *down* (= make her decide) to anything./ Many modern floor coverings are *stapled down* with industrial staplers./ The badly-injured patient had to be *strapped down* so that he could not move./ The edge of the carpet is turning up; it needs to be *tacked down*./ John is a bad patient. To keep him in bed I almost have to *tie/hold* him *down*./ I would like to leave this job but I am *tied down* (= restricted) by a contract.

b **to argue, to cry, to hoot, to laugh, to shout, to talk**

These verbs are used with **down** to indicate that the action prevents another person from talking etc.

When one of the workers moved that the strike be called off, the others *argued/cried/hooted/shouted* him *down*./ When the MP is the House of Commons commended the Government for its admirable policies, the Opposition *laughed* her *down*./ Whenever I tried to say something at the meeting the chairman *talked* me *down*.

c to calm, to cool, to die, to quieten, to settle, to simmer

I was afraid that their yacht would capsize, but the wind has *calmed down* now./ I was extremely angry with Jane this morning but now I have *calmed down*./ I'll be glad when this hot weather *cools down*./ The chairman said, 'Now that everyone has *cooled/simmered down*, perhaps we can discuss this matter without losing our tempers.'/ The wind has *died down* (= ceased gradually)./ There were rumours that the prince was to marry a film star, but when nothing happened, they soon *died down*./ The baby is crying again; I'll go and try to *settle* him *down*./ My stomach was upset this morning but it has *settled down* now and I feel much better./ Many young people like to knock about a bit before they decide to *settle down*.

d to run

The clock has *run down* (= stopped), wind it up./ There is no sense in overworking and letting your health *run down* (= deteriorate)./ He had a good little business but when he took to drinking too much he let it *run down*./ The thieves in the car tried to *run* the policeman *down* (= knock him over with the car)./ The detectives *ran* the criminals *down* (= caught them) as they were about to cross over to France./ Jane seldom has a good word to say for anyone; she's always *running* people *down* (= criticizing them).

e to break

My car *broke down* yesterday so I had to come by bus today./ The government's plan to help pensioners is in danger of *breaking down* (= ceasing to work)./ The old lady *broke down* (= lost control of her emotions) and wept when she heard that her son had had a serious accident./ The statistician said 'If we *break down* (= analyse) these figures we'll find some interesting facts.'/ Various chemicals in the soil are *broken down* (= reduced to their constituent parts) by bacteria.

f to grind, to fight, to pack, to put

Grind the nutmeg *down* to a powder. Before the Revolution the French peasants were *ground down* (= cruelly oppressed) by the rich landowners./ The teacher *fought down* her rising anger with the girl./ He *fought down* a feeling of nausea./ You can get a lot more in that suitcase if you *pack* the stuff *down*./ He filled the hole with earth and *packed* it *down*./ He *put* the cup of coffee *down* on the table./ The government troops *put down* (= subdued) the rebellion with great severity./ The authorities made an effort to *put down* organized crime in the city./ The racehorse broke a leg and was *put down* (killed painlessly)./

Other functions of *down*

g to back, to climb (= to change one's mind because of fear or uncertainty)

When I took up his offer to play a tennis match for £10.00 he *backed down*./ The strikers *backed down* when they were threatened with the sack. When I showed him he was wrong he *climbed down* and said he was sorry.

to bog

After the heavy rains, many cars were *bogged down* in the mud on the country roads./ The peace negotiations between the two warring countries are *bogged down* (= have ceased to progress).

to boil, to burn

If you put those bones in a pot and *boil* them *down*, they'll make good soup./ I think all your advice *boils down* (= is reduced) to this — that I declare myself bankrupt./ Whatever you say about John, it all *boils down* to the fact that he is lazy./ The family had to move because their house was *burned down*.

to close

This radio station is now *closing down*./ The ship had a notice on the window saying 'Closing-down sale'.

to live (= to behave so that past faults are forgotten)

Bill would like to forget the time he got drunk and made a fool of himself but his friends won't let him *live* it *down*./ He did his best to *live down* the fact that he had once been in prison.

to let (= to disappoint)

John was going to help me but he *let* me *down*.

to narrow

The police *narrowed down* the number of suspects in the murder case to two./ If we have a lot of choices we have to *narrow* them *down*.

to nestle, to snuggle

It was such a cold morning, that instead of getting up he *nestled/snuggled down* in his bed and went back to sleep.

to turn

Mary was offered a good job but she *turned* it *down* (= refused it). He wanted to join the army but was *turned down* because of his health.

to track

Trained dogs are used for *tracking down* wild pigs and other animals./ The cause of this illness is still unknown but one day the scientists will *track* it *down* (= discover it).

h There is a group of verbs with which the particle down conveys not only a mixture of the completive and directional senses but also the sense of something vertical, e.g. a building, a wall, a person etc, falling to the ground.
to blow, to break, to bring, to chop, to fall, to hack, to hew, to knock, to mow (fig.), to pull, to ride, to shoot, to slash, to strike, to topple, to tumble

The strong wind *blew/knocked down* many trees../ The police had to *break down* the door to get into the house./ That fence is not very strong; any wind will *bring* it *down*./ That old wall is dangerous; it may *fall/topple down* any day./ *The developers just chopped/hacked/hewed down* all the trees to make way for new buildings./ Old-time gangsters got rid of their enemies by *gunning/shooting* them *down*./ Many buildings were made unsafe by the earthquake and had to be *knocked/pulled/torn/down*./ Barbara is in hospital, she was *knocked down* by a car./ The badly-armed revolutionaries were *mown down* by machine gun fire./ When the farmer tried to stop the horseman he was *ridden down*./ The unfortunate man was *struck down* by lightning during the storm./ May God *strike* me *down* if I am not telling the truth./ There is a well-known poem which says 'Sceptre and crown must *tumble down*, and in the vile dust be equal made to the poor crooked scythe and spade.'

i Down is also used to convey a sense of lessening, reducing in size, amount strength, intensity etc.
to cut, to file, to melt, to pare, to rub, to slow, to thin, to tone, to water, to wear

The woman *cut down* her husband's old trousers to make clothes for her son./ You really must *cut down* on your smoking (= smoke less)./ This locking pin won't fit into the hole, I'll have to *file* it *down*./ The company bought old metal, *melted* it *down* and sold it for re-use./ The government had a campaign to *pare down* expenditure in the civil service./ Before he varnished it he *rubbed* the table *down* with fine sandpaper./ In the second half the pace of the match began to *slow down*./ You are too fat. You need some exercise to *thin* you *down* a bit./ *Tone* your voices *down*, the baby is asleep./ The management told the strikers that, if they *toned* their demands *down*, they might be met./ The milkman was fined for *watering down* his milk./ The account published in the papers of the scandal was *watered down* (= made to seem less shocking than it really was)./ These shoes are badly *worn down* at the heels./ The police *wore* the suspect *down* (reduced his/her resistance) by their continual questioning.

j **to climb, to do, to let, to step**

When I showed him he was wrong he *climbed down* (= retracted his statement) and said he was sorry./ That shopkeeper will *do* you *down* (= cheat you) if he gets the chance./ Frank was going to help me but he *let* me *down* (= disappointed me)./ The chairman was getting old so he decided to *step down* to make way for a younger person.

k **to brush, to hose, to nib, to wash, to wipe**
Down is often used to refer to the cleaning of large areas, objects or living bodies.

You've got dust on your suit. Just a minute and I'll *brush* you *down*./ You'll have to *hose* that car *down* to get the mud off./ The horse was covered with sweat and had to be *rubbed down*./ That glass door is covered with finger marks; *wash/wipe* it *down*.

Exercises

1 *In each space below put either an appropriate particle or an appropriate verb. Discuss any alternatives:*

1 'What shall I do with these books?' 'First wrap them . . . . . . , then box them . . . . . . and make sure the lids of the boxes are . . . . . . down.'

2 The shopkeeper said, 'Business is bad. It's the same everywhere. It just . . . . . . down to the fact that people don't have enough money to spend. Anything they have saved . . . . . . , they use for essentials. I think I'll be forced to . . . . . . down. If I sell . . . . . . now I may not lose quite so much.'

3 The strikers' negotiations with the factory management are getting nowhere. They have got . . . . . . down. But I think that the strikers will be forced to . . . . . . down as they haven't worked for more than a month.

4 That car of mine is always . . . . . . down. I think that it's only good enough for breaking . . . . . . for spare parts.

5 I hate receiving parcels that are . . . . . . down with sellotape. I get so angry having to struggle to open them that it takes me several minutes to . . . . . . down.

6 Some students get so wound . . . . . . before examinations that they take tranquillizing pills to . . . . . . themselves down.

7 The cargo on the deck of a ship has to be . . . . . . down so that it won't move . . . . . . during a storm.

8 The climbers set . . . . . . with great hopes of reaching the summit but next day they were . . . . . . down by a fierce blizzard.

9 Our body . . . . . . down the foods we eat into the essential substances it needs.

10 The manager of the large department store said, 'Our security staff will have to wake themselves . . . . . . We're losing thousands of pounds a week to shoplifters. They come in here and walk . . . . . . with all sorts of goods. Some of them would steal anything that's not . . . . . . down. From now on we're going to . . . . . . down on all this.'

11 When the publicity surrounding her marriage had . . . . . . down the film star and her husband . . . . . . down on a small farm in the country.

2 *In each space below put one of these particles:* **up, down, off, about around, out.**

1 The campers did not peg their tent . . . . . . carefully and it kept flapping . . . . . . in the wind.
2 Those pots and pans are still hot. Let them cool . . . . . . before you scrape them . . . .
3 The young couple were very cut . . . . . . when their house was burnt . . . . . . and, because they were behind in their insurance payments, the company refused to pay . . . .
4 Many young men don't get married early because they don't want to be tied . . . . . . by a family. They want to be free to knock . . . . . . a bit first and also to save something . . . . . . for the future.
5 What a terrible week-end we had. To start . . . . . . the car broke . . . . . . when we were only half way to Cornwall. John eventually got it going again but he was in such a temper that it took him hours to simmer . . . . When we went to book in at the hotel we found that it was full . . . . We found another but the hotel keeper tried to do us . . . .
6 George said that he would back me . . . . . . when I asked the boss for a rise but when the time came to make . . . . . . his mind he backed . . . .
7 The patrol, which was ordered . . . . . . to blow . . . . . . the bridge, was pinned . . . . . . on the hillside by enemy fire and they fought . . . . . . several determined attacks. They were expecting some reinforcements from their own side to back them . . . . . . but they did not come and eventually the patrol was wiped . . . .
8 When Jean began her new office job she started . . . . . . by being full of enthusiasm but in no time she was fed . . . . . . with the routine. She said that most of her time was taken . . . . . . with messing . . . . . . with bits of paper. The only thing she looked forward to each day was the time to knock . . . . . . She felt really let . . . .

3 *Try to answer these questions using phrasal verbs. Use your imagination and make your answers as full as possible. Use not only the phrasal verbs discussed above but also verbs from previous sections of the book. Work in pairs.*

1 If you want me to post these books on the table to Mary, tell me what to do.

2 If you try to drive a car on muddy country roads what might happen? And then what would you have to do to the car when you get home?
3 I hear that you went away camping in your car last week-end. Tell me what happened.
4 What sometimes happens to people who work too hard and worry a lot?
5 How can I stop that loose floorboard from squeaking?
6 Why is that shop having a sale at this time of the year?
7 Why do people insure their houses?
8 If people lose their tempers in an argument what is the best thing to do?
9 If too many people start breaking the law what is likely to happen?
10 What are some of the disadvantages of marrying young?

4 *Choose the right verb or particle from those given in brackets.*

1 The girl was very tired. She (quietened/calmed/nestled/bogged/backed) down in the comfortable armchair and in no time she had drifted (away/out/about/down/off).
2 As a result of the atomic bomb attacks on Japan thousands of people were (wiped/washed/cleaned/swept/rubbed) out and cities burnt (away/up/off/around/down).
3 In large cities old buildings are always being (shut/put/run/chopped/torn) down and new ones being (sent/blown/put/given/made) up.
4 That storm last night has really messed (away/down/out/up/over) my garden. Most of my new plants have been (blown/fallen/struck/ground/put) down and all they need now is a heavy frost to (send/die/kill/make) them off.
5 Jane seems to see the bad side of people and she (sends/runs/knocks/grinds/ties) them down whereas Barbara tends to (live/clean/act/blow/build) people up because she sees their good side.
6 The biologist searching for the cause of the strange illness refused to (give/blow/close/wrap/end) up. He was sure that he could (tack/glue/pin/stick/hold) it down to something relatively simple.
7 When Joe was young and unmarried he used to live it (away/about/down/up/off) a bit but now that he has married and (nestled/bogged/pinned/glued/settled) down, he is anxious to (live/put/break/mow/knock) down his early reputation for high living. He even (put/ground/banked/turned/broke) down my invitation to the party last week.

8 Although at first the youth (closed/shut/clammed/glued/stuck) up when the police questioned him about the robbery, after further questioning he broke (off/up/down/about/in) and (gave/made/opened/acted/owned) up.
9 The poor peasants of the Middle Ages often became (choked/fattened/bottled/fed/cut) up with the way they were ground (about/up/off/down/away) by the rich land owners so that they would (rise/fly/stand/drive/give) up against their masters but these uprisings were (sent/put/knocked/cut/mown) down with great severity.
10 When one of the strikers spoke up and said he thought that they were (building/making/raking/piling/rounding) up a minor dispute into a major issue he was shouted (off/away/about/up/down) by the meeting and there were cries of, '(Close/Clam/Hush/Belt/Finish) up!'

5 *Replace each group of italicized words with a suitable phrasal verb. You may have to supply an object. Discuss any losses or gains in brevity, formality, emphasis, clarity etc. between the two sentences. Also discuss any alternatives.*

1 I was feeling rather annoyed with him so I told him to *keep quiet.*
2 English people are supposed to be the sort of people who *suppress their feelings.*
3 I managed to *overcome with some difficulty* my rising feeling of anger.
4 The pet dog was very old and very ill and his owner reluctantly agreed to have him *put to sleep.*
5 There were a lot of rich people *leading lives of luxury and extravagance* on the French Riviera.
6 When a government member got up to answer the charge the opposition *made such a loud noise that he could not be heard.*
7 When the woman heard that the operation on her little daughter had been successful she *could control her emotions no longer.*
8 I tried to help Bill stop drinking many times but in the end I just *ceased trying.*
9 The flap of the envelope must be *fixed firmly with glue.*
10 I am afraid that the City Council's campaign to *take firm measures against* people who throw litter about the streets has *ceased to be effective any longer.*
11 Those old buildings have been *demolished* and new ones have been *erected.*

12 Kings and princes must *fall from their exalted places* and in the grave be made equal to the humblest peasant.
13 After many years of *moving from place to place* he decided to get married and *live quietly in one place*.
14 I haven't yet been able to find that piece of information you wanted but I'll *keep looking until I find it* for you.
15 When the man heard that his home had been *destroyed by fire* he *was very emotionally upset*.

6 *Try to answer these questions using any of the phrasal verbs with* **down** *discussed in the last two sections and as many other phrasal verbs as you can. Work in pairs.*

1 If young children get over-excited, what should we do to them?
2 What happened at the meeting when George tried to object to the motion?
3 What do you do on a cold winter's morning when it is a holiday and you don't have to get up?
4 I know that Fred was rather wild when he was young and served several short prison sentences but what is he doing with himself now?
5 Why can't you get Anne to make up her mind about a date for the club meeting?
6 I saw you come home in a taxi yesterday. What happened? Something wrong with your car?
7 What usually happens if a small business like a shop goes bankrupt?
8 What may happen if you have people who are very careless smokers living in your house?

13 The use of the particles *in* and *out* to denote inclusion and exclusion

a These two particles can be used with the same verb to form a pair of opposites.

to be, to count, to keep, to leave, to phase, to want

We have a Christmas raffle for a large turkey. Do you want to *be in?*/'*Are* you still *in* the golf tournament?' 'No I'm not. Jones beat me.'/ The company decided that they too wanted to *be in* on the big government contracts./ If you're going for a holiday to Greece this year, *count* me *in*, but if it's only Bournemouth *count* me *out*./ Violet's a good committee member; let's *keep* her *in*./ We don't want Nicholas on the committee. Let's do our best to *keep* him *out*./ *Leave* me *in*; don't take my name off the list./ We don't want Julian at the party; *leave* him *out*./ The machinery at present in the factory will be *phased* out (= excluded in stages) over the next three years./ To avoid confusion the new work schedule will be *phased in* over a month./ When we first discussed our new investment scheme, Bill said that he *wanted in* but when we tried to pin him down he said that he *wanted out* (= wished to be excluded — mainly US usage).

b Some verbs when used the with the particle can convey the idea of including a forgotten detail, note, or of completing a form. etc.

to chalk, to draw, to fill, to ink, to mark, to paint, to pencil, to write

You've left Tuesday's appointment out of your diary. I'll just *mark/pencil/write* it in for you./ I hte *filling in* my income tax forms. The picture's not quite finished; there are a few small details that need to be *inked/painted/chalked/pencilled/drawn in*.

c Other verbs use with **in** to denote inclusion are
to cut, to deal, to dig, to get (on), to horn (on), to join, to muscle, to pitch, to scrape, to sit (on)

I see you're playing poker. Will you *cut/deal* me *in* (= include me in the game)./ I wish our company would *cut* its employees *in* on some of the enormous profits they are making./ John's not good enough for the tennis team. I don't think he'll *get in*./ David says he has a foolproof investment scheme and that now's the time to *get in* on the big money./ The juniors were having a quiet game of football and the seniors came and *horned/muscled in* (= included themselves by force)./ All the other children play nicely together but Billy doesn't seem to want to *join in*./ We're having an impromptu party; come and *join in*./ Look at all these dishes we have to *wash up*. If we all *pitch in* (= co-operate) we'll soon get them done./ Mrs Smith is *rounding up* people to take part in a Christmas play. If you're not careful you'll be *roped in* (= made to make part)./ 'Did your candidate get elected to Parliament?' 'Yes, he just *scraped in* by a few votes (= he only just got in).' The headmaster said 'I see you're taking history Miss Allot, do you mind if I *sit in* for a short while?'/ I went and *sat in* on (= was present at) one of the local council meetings last week.

d Verbs used with **out** to denote exclusion are
to chicken, to contract, to cross, to cut, to drop, to freeze, to opt, to pull, to rule, to strike

Julia said that she was going to be part of our deputation to the management but now she has *chickened out* (= changed her mind because she is afraid)./ When he discovered that the business deal was illegal he decided to *contract out* (= disassociate himself)./ I don't want to be in; *cross/strike* my name *out*./ Jeremy was friendly with Valerie until Andrew came along and *cut* him *out* (= took his place)./ Emily *dropped/pulled out* of the championship because of an attack of flu./ After he was involved in that scandal about money the members of Alan's club just *froze* him *out* (= excluded him)./ The big supermarkets are *freezing* small grocers *out* of business./ The business man said to his partner 'If you do anything that brings us into conflict with the law, I shall *opt out*.'/ We'll have to *rule out* expansion for next year — our profits aren't big enough./ Professional athletes are *ruled out* of the Olympic games.

73

Exercises

1 *For each sentence below supply a phrasal verb with* **in** *or* **out.**

1 I don't like John and, if he's going to the party, you can
. . . . . . me . . . .

2 The larger traders in the street tried to . . . . . . the small businessman . . . . . . but he survived in spite of their efforts.

3 The American tourist in France said, 'Now, I've come this far I
may as well . . . . . . Britain as well.'

4 The American said, 'We're playing poker. If you want to play, sit
down and I'll . . . . . . you . . . .'

5 Jane's not as brave as she pretends to be. She keeps saying that
she's going to tell the boss this and that but when the opportunity
arises she . . . .

6 'I've got all this mess to clean up but if you . . . . . . and help it'll
be done in half the time.'

7 'Why is Jane going out with Fred? I thought she was Joe's girl-
riend.' 'Well, she used to be but Fred . . . . . . him . . . .'

8 'Do you think you'll be accepted for university this year?' 'Well,
I'm not too hopeful but with luck I might . . . .'

9 I said that I'd come with you on holiday to Las Palmas but on
further thought I think I'll . . . . . . as I can't afford it.

10 You left Janet's name off the list so I've just . . . . . . it . . . .

11 Everybody seemed to be having a good time at the carnival so we
all decided to . . . .

12 Jack seems to be making a lot of money out of that new business
he started; I wish I could . . . . . . of it myself.

2 *Put* **in, out, down** *or* **up** *in each space below.*

1 'Hello John. Good to see you. Come . . . . . . for a few minutes
and sit . . . . . . I suppose you want to see Jane. She's upstairs but
she'll be . . . . . . in a few minutes. In fact you're lucky to find her
. . . . . . as she's just dressing herself . . . . . . to go . . . . . . with
that new boy-friend of hers. Anyway I'm glad you called
. . . . . . because I'd like to talk to you. A group of us are trying
to round . . . . . . a few interested people to raise money for the
children's home. It's quite a simple thing and won't take
. . . . . . much of your time. We're having a meeting tomorrow
night and perhaps you'd like to come along and sit . . . . . . on it
without committing yourself. There's no point in your saying 'yes'
until you've made . . . . . . your mind. Anyway, give it some
thought.'

2 The present government has decided to cut . . . . . . the number
of semi-governmental organizations. Some are to be closed
. . . . . . immediately but others are to be phased . . . . . . over a
period. A special committee is to be set . . . . . . to carry out this
work.

3 The government spokesman said that the British economic team
were trying to set . . . . . . a meeting with the French economic
team but so far they had not been able to pin the French
. . . . . . to a suitable date. He said, however, that the government
would not give . . . . . . trying to complete the arrangements as
they did not want relations between the two countries to
. . . . . . down at this stage.

4 One of the clerks thought that he would like to get . . . . . . on
some of the profits that his bank was making. He did this by
carefully choosing certain cheques and inking . . . . . . significant
alterations. He became so confident that he did not even rule
. . . . . . the possibility of being able to steal £1 000 000. Suspicions
however were aroused when he was seen to be living it . . . . . .
at certain expensive night spots. When he discovered that the bank
authorities had been doing some checking . . . . . . he decided to
own . . . . . . to everything and give the money back. He was
lucky and got off rather lightly. The bank hushed the whole epi-
sode . . . . . . because they knew that, if the newspapers got hold
of it, they would build it . . . . . . into a sensation that would do
the bank no good.

5 The inhabitants of the small village had made . . . . . . their minds
that the nearby volcano had quietened . . . . . . and was unlikely
to act . . . . . . again. But, when they were woken . . . . . . in the
middle of the night to find their houses tumbling . . . . . . about
their ears, they realized how mistaken they had been. Although
nearly all the houses were knocked . . . . . . fortunately no one
was killed. A few days later a government official arrived to try to
sum . . . . . . the damage. The villagers wanted to know what sort
of help they would get from the government but the official would
not be pinned . . . . . . The villagers became angry and said that
his attitude boiled . . . . . . to the fact that the central government
had always ground them . . . . . . with heavy taxes, even forcing
them to pay . . . . . . when they could least afford it. Any request
for aid was always turned . . . . . . The official managed to calm
them . . . . . . by assuring them that, if any aid was available, they
would not be left . . . .

3 *Choose the correct phrasal verb from those given in brackets.*

1 I don't like Bournemouth. If you are thinking of going there for a holiday you can (count/opt/contract/phase/freeze) me out.
2 The President of the USA said that military action to free the hostages could not be (opted/left/crossed/ruled/chickened) out.
3 There are a few branches of the business that are not very profitable and during the next year they will be (crossed/phased/left/counted/contracted) out.
4 The American businessman said, 'It sounds to me like a good proposition and I (muscle/deal/count/write/want) in.'
5 There was a gang war among the criminals because one group tried to (scrape/rope/muscle/deal/sit) in on another's illegal activities.
6 'Did Jane try to (scrape/rope/want/join/pitch) you in to make a four at bridge tonight?'
7 The four girls lived together in the flat and they (pitched/opted/sat/cut/were) in to do the work and pay the bills.
8 'We want a few more people to come on the trip to Paris next weekend.' 'Well, I (count/opt/get/be/take) in already, so ask John.'

4 *In each of the sentences below replace the italicized words by a phrasal verb from those discussed in this section. Discuss any changes as previously.*

1 Some of the older boys tried to *force their way uninvited into* the party that the younger boys at the school had organized.
2 John joined the hang-gliding club because he said he was keen to learn but when one of his friends was injured he *was afraid* and did not continue.
3 The painter said that the picture was almost finished. There were only a few small details that he had to *add with his brush.*
4 'Do you think you'll get in the football team this year?'
  'Well, I might just *manage to be selected.*'
5 Some children love games but others are too shy to *participate.*
6 Miss Jones, I've been checking this list and I find that you have *omitted* several items.
7 This side of the business has proved unprofitable so we have decided to *get rid of it gradually* over the next six months.
8 Miss Jones, where is my desk diary? I want you to *add with a pencil* that appointment that I have next week.

5 *Try to answer these questions using phrasal verbs from the above section and any other phrasal verbs that you can. Work in pairs.*

1 If you see your friends enjoying themselves what should you do?
2 f someone offered you the chance to make a lot of money, what would you say to them?
3 If your friends were going to do something of which you didn't approve and you didn't wish to join in, what would you say?
4 If your friends were planning something of which you did approve and you wanted to join in, what would you say?
5 If your friends were having a game of cards which you wanted to join in, what would you ask?
6 If someone asked you why you thought that geography was such a wide subject, what would you answer?
7 Why didn't George go mountain climbing with you last week-end?
8 Look at George talking to Bill's girlfriend. What do you think he's trying to do?
9 I can't see your name on the list, John. What do you think has happened?
10 What sort of result did your candidate get in the parliamentary elections?

14 Further uses of the particles *in* and *out*

a The particle **in** can be used to express the idea of *at home, inside, indoors, on the premises* (e.g. office, hotel etc.), *in this place*.
The particle **out** can express *away from home, outside, out of doors away from the premises, in another place*.
The verbs which can be used with these two particles to form pairs of opposites are
to be, to dine, to eat, to find, to live, to lock, to shut, to sleep, to stay, to stop, to take

I'll *be in* at 8 o'clock tonight./ It's your birthday tomorrow — let's *eat*/*dine out* (= at a restaurant)./ If you go to his office now, you might *find* him *in*./ Quite a few of the hotel staff *lived in* (= on the premises)./ When Jamie *stayed out* till three in the morning his wife *locked* him *out*./ If I work late at the hotel I can *sleep in* but I usually prefer to *sleep out*./ I didn't get in till 3 o'clock this morning so I'm afraid I *slept in* (= stayed in bed) until noon./ I wouldn't care to be homeless and have to *sleep out* in this cold weather./ I'm tired this morning; I *stayed*/*stopped out* too late last night./ Grandfather likes to be *taken out* for a walk every afternoon./ Alice was brought up by Mrs Evans who *took* her *in* when her parents died.

b **In** can also be used to convey a sense of restriction of action or movement. In this case the particle is generally used with a verb of building, constructing or enclosing.
to belt, to box, to buckle, to build, to bunch, to close, to crowd, to fence, to hedge, to hem, to ice (usually pass.), **to shut, to snow** (usually pass.), **to strap, to wall**

Drivers of racing cars are usually *belted*/*buckled*/*strapped in*./ Our house is now *boxed in* by high buildings./ When I *lived in* a small bedsit in London I felt so *boxed in*./ The runner was *bunched in* by a number of others and was unable to get past them./ I don't like living in the city, I feel so *closed/shut in*./ In the London underground at rush hours passengers are *crowded in* like sardines./ The words of an old song say 'Give me land, lots of land . . . don't *fence me in*./ Government officials do not have much freedom of action; they are *hedged in* by rules and regulations./ Tibet is *hemmed in* by high mountains. The Greeks at Marathon kept fighting although they were *hemmed in* (= surrounded and trapped) by the Persians./ The ships of the Arctic expedition were *iced in* for many months./ The people who live in the far north of Canada are *snowed in* for quite a few months each year./ The small garden had been *walled in* to make it private.

c **Out** is used with some verbs to convey the sense of distribution or issuing.
to deal, to dish, to dole, to farm, to give, to hand, to hire, to mete, to parcel, to pass, to pay, to put, to rent, to send, to serve, to share

'Let's start the game. Come on, *deal* the cards *out*.'/ At the Christmas party Uncle Edmund was *dishing/doling/serving out* large helpings of ice-cream to all the children./ The world champion heavyweight boxer *dishes out* terrible punishment to his opponents./ The teacher was fond of *doling/dealing out* punishment to the class for the smallest fault./ The company had only a small clothing factory but it *farmed out* a lot of work to women working at home./ At the meeting the chairman *gave/handed/passed out* copies of the annual report./ At the Salvation Army mission warm clothes were *given/handed/passed out* to the poor./ Peter *hires out* fishing rods and boats for an hour at a time./ Some people believe than an angry god *metes out* punishment to sinners./ In the early days of the USA the government *parcelled out* (= distributed shares of) land to settlers./ This company *pays out* over £5000 a week in wages./ The company is going to *put out* a new magazine for children./ The farmer *rented out* some cottages to holiday makers./ The aeroplane *sent out* a distress signal./ Miss Andrews, have you *sent* those circulars *out* yet (= distributed them)?/Oliver, don't eat all those sweets; *share* them *out* among your friends.

Exercises

1 *In each space in the sentences below put a suitable phrasal verb from those discussed above. You may have to supply an object for the verb. Discuss any alternatives.*

1 I've been trying to see Jane for weeks. I went around to her house at 6 p.m. last night hoping to . . . . . . but she was out.
2 The clerk lived in a small boarding house in London but the food was so bad that he usually . . . .
3 'Why are you so late home from school tonight, Billy?'
   'I didn't do my homework and the teacher . . . .'
4 When I was a boy scout I used to love the week-ends when we went into the country and . . . . . . under the trees and by the streams.
5 I must go home. My mother doesn't like me to . . . . . . too late at night.

2 *In each space in the sentences below put a suitable phrasal verb from those discussed above. You may have to supply a object for the verb. Discuss any alternatives.*

1 I live in the country and whenever I visit my sister who lives in a small flat in the city I feel so . . . .
2 I was so . . . . . . by other people on the bus last night that I couldn't get out and had to go past my stop.
3 Before starting off, the driver made sure that he was properly . . . .
4 'That's a nice little garden at the back of your house.'
   'Yes, I think I'll . . . . . . to make it more private.'
5 The general said, 'The enemy troops are moving to our rear and, if we don't withdraw, we'll be . . . .'

3 *In each space in the sentences below put a suitable phrasal verb those discussed above. You may have to supply an object for the verb. Discuss any alternatives.*

1 At the end of his lecture the professor . . . . . . some typed notes to the students.
2 The government printing agency . . . . . . a lot of its work to private contractors.
3 Private detectives . . . . . . their services to those who can afford to pay for them.

4 Ancient rulers were often feared by their subjects because they had the power to . . . . . . the severest of punishments.
5 Janet wanted to have a big 21st birthday party and she . . . . . . invitations to all her friends.
6 The Japanese are . . . . . . a great number of new electronic devices this year.

4 *In the spaces in the sentences below put either a suitable verb or a suitable particle.*

1 Last night we decided to dine . . . . . . at a Chinese restaurant that had been recommended to us but when we got there we found that the place had . . . . . . down and so we wound . . . . . . by eating at a nearby Indian restaurant.
2 The Alpine village was . . . . . . in by high mountains and often during a severe winter the inhabitants were snowed . . . . . . for weeks on end.
3 During the Middle Ages mercenary soldiers would . . . . . . their skills out to whoever paid the most. Many rulers and petty princes whose main aim seemed to be to grind their subjects . . . . . . often used these soldiers to . . . . . . down rebellions among their discontented subjects.
4 I was supposed to go . . . . . . with Bill last night but I . . . . . . up an excuse not to go because I wanted to stay . . . . . . and tidy . . . . . . my room. I also wanted to brush . . . . . . some maths for the test tomorrow.
5 Henry VIII of England parcelled . . . . . . the church lands among those who had . . . . . . him up in his argument with the Pope.
6 At the university, degrees are not just . . . . . . out, you know. Right from the start you've got to . . . . . . up your mind to work hard because, if you don't measure . . . . . . it's quite likely you'll . . . . . . up by getting kicked . . . .'
7 'What a nice garden you have. I didn't know you had taken . . . . . . gardening.'
'Well, I haven't . . . . . . it up seriously. I really only potter . . . . . . One day I . . . . . . up a small piece of ground and put . . . . . . a few seeds which just happened to come . . . . . . , and that's how it started. Also, my doctor said I was working too hard and had to slow . . . . . . or I'd . . . . . . up with a nervous breakdown. So, gardening is good for me.'
8 The official said, 'Many of these regulations are too strict. I often find it impossible to . . . . . . up my mind about anything because

I am so tied . . . . . by petty rules and regulations. I'm afraid that this is the reason why so many of our plans get . . . . . . down, and we get nowhere.'

5 *Put one of these phrasal verbs with* **stay** *in each sentence below make sure that the verbs are in the right form.*

to stay in, to stay out, to stay about/around, to stay down, to stay away

1 'Is Fred a friend of yours, Mary?'
  'No, he isn't. He's a nuisance. He's always coming around to the house and asking for me. I just wish he would go away and . . . .'
2 Janet should have been home by midnight last night but she . . . . . . until 2 a.m.
3 'Let's go home now — coming?' 'No, I think I'll . . . . . . for a while and see if I can get another game of tennis.'
4 I was very sick after that barbecue last week. Everything I ate came up again. Then for several days afterwards nothing I ate would . . . . . .
5 'There's something wrong with this screw. It won't . . . . . . Every time I screw it in it falls out.'

6 *Put one of these phrasal verbs with* **take** *in each sentence below (make sure that the verbs are in the right form)* **to take in, to take out, to take about/around, to take down, to take off.**

1 The flag is usually raised at sunrise and . . . . . . at sunset.
2 When I visited Amsterdam last year a Dutch friend of mine . . . . . . me . . . . . . in his car.
3 I went to the library yesterday and . . . . . . four novels.
4 In the Christmas story, Joseph found there was 'no room at the inn' because no one would . . . . . . his family . . . .
5 At the world's great airports planes are . . . . . . and coming down every few seconds.

7 *Try to answer these questions using phrasal verbs from the above section and any other phrasal verbs that you can. Work in pairs.*

1 What did you do last night. Did you go out?
2 'I don't think that I would like to live in one of those small Alpine villages' 'Why not?'
3 I see that you have a lot of healthy seedlings coming up in your hothouse. What are you going to do with them?

4 'It's our wedding anniversary tomorrow, dear. What would you like to do to celebrate?'

5 What was it like when you were a student living in a small room in the centre of London?

6 If a factory had too many orders and could not fill them, what could it do with the extra work?

7 I hear you are working at the Grand Hotel. Where do you live and what do you do for your meals?

8 'If you want our candidate to get in, take these pamphlets.'
'But what do you want me to do with them?'

9 That farmer has a lot of small cottages on his property. What do you think he does with them?

10 Now that you've written these invitations, what do you want me to do with them?

Verbs used with *out* in the completive sense

a to conk, to die, to fizzle, to give, to pass, to peter, to run
Most of these verbs convey the idea of ceasing gradually.

Our old TV set suddenly *conked out* last night, so we missed the last part of the serial. It's not worth getting it mended, we're going to buy a new one./ Many minor languages have now *died out* (= become extinct)./ The road safety campaign *fizzled out* through lack of public interest./ John begins things full of enthusiasm but it soon *fizzles out*./ Ruth came back from France because her money *gave/ ran out*./ The teacher was very angry; his patience had *given/run out*./ Whenever I see blood I tend to *pass out* (= become unconscious)./ The snowed-in climbers found that their supplies were *petering out*./

b to black, to blanket, to blot, to drown, to stamp, to wipe
These verbs convey the idea of obliteration.

When an electricity generator failed half the city was *blacked out*./ In wartime, cities are *blacked out* as a protection against air raids./ When I fell down and hit my head I *blacked out* (= became unconscious) for a few seconds./ This fog is awful; it *blankets out* everything and makes driving very difficult./ Our view of the sea has been *blotted out* by a high block of flats./ Hypnosis can *blot out* a person's memory of certain actions or happenings./ During the war aerial bombing *blotted out* parts of the town./ The speaker's voice was *drowned out* by the drone of an aeroplane passing overhead./ The hunter *stamped out* the embers of the campfire with his heavy boots./ The world's police are co-operating to *stamp out* (= abolish) the drug traffic./ She saw that a cigarette butt in the ashtray was still glowing so she picked it up and *stubbed* it *out*.

c to beat, to flatten, to hammer, to iron, to smooth, to straighten

I must have those darts *beaten/hammered out of my car./ The army chiefs of staff got together and hammered out* (= formed after hard work and discussion) a plan of campaign./ When the plane attacked the soldiers *flattened* themselves *out* on the ground./ She *ironed/smoothed* the creases *out* of her dress./ The Foreign Secretary said 'There are certain differences of opinion between us and our allies which need to be *ironed/smoothed out./* Once I saw a man bend an iron bar and then *straighten* it *out* with his bare hands./ That class has been a very difficult one but I think the new teacher will *straighten* them *out. (fig.* = make them behave./ When people get wrong first impressions of a country it takes some time to *straighten* them *out* (= give them the right ideas)./ The rich man died without a will and it took the lawyers a long time to *straighten out* his affairs.

d to map, to measure, to mark, to pace, to step, to weigh

The whole area had been *mapped out* by the air force./ Giles' parents are very wealthy and they've *mapped* his future (= *out* (= planned). The distance from the gate to the garage is 20 metres; I *measured* it *out./* The housewife carefully *weighed/measured out* the ingredients for her cake./ The workers *marked out* a badminton court on the factory floor./ 'How long is this room?' 'I don't know, but let's *pace/step* it *out.*'

e to catch, to find, to make, to root, to smell, to sort, to work

When we played poker yesterday Pip tried to cheat but I *caught* him *out* (= discovered him doing it)./ I have just *found out* (= discovered) that Emma was married yesterday./ Will you *find out* for me when the plane takes off tomorrow?/ In the fog I could just *make out* (= see) the white lines on the road./ Why did John throw up that good job? I can't *make* it *out* (= understand)./ These shrubs are no good; I think I'll *root* them all *out* (= dig them up)./ The new police chief is determined to *root out* (= get rid off) corruption./ I will *root out* the truth if I have to interview everyone in this class./ Customs officials use specially-trained dogs who can *smell out* certain drugs./ If there is any scandal in the district Mrs Jones is sure to *smell* it *out./* Sort out the bad apples from that box and we'll *throw* them *out./* My tax affairs are in such a mess that I'll have to get an accountant to *sort* them *out.*

f to brush, to clean, to dust, to hose, to scrape, to scrub, to swab, to sweep, to tidy

These are all verbs of cleaning

Brush out that drawer for me./ I must *hose out* the garage./ *Scrape out* those pots./ He decided to *scrub out* the kitchen./ The doctor *swabbed out* the wound./ That room's filthy; I'd better *sweep* it *out*./ Could you *tidy out* those drawers?

Other verbs with *out*

to be

I'm out of cash (= have none left)./ Fred *is out* of work.

to bear

The accused man said, 'The witness will *bear out* what I claimed, that I was at home when the crime was committed./ I am not lying, this man will *bear* me *out*.

to blow

He lit a match but the wind *blew* it *out*./ Arabella had an accident this morning when her two front tyres *blew out* (= exploded and deflated).

to burn

A large office building was *burnt out* last — only the outside walls were left./ The campfire *burnt* itself *out*./ If you work too hard you'll *burn* yourself *out* (*fig.*).

to buy

Simon used to have 30 per cent of the shares in the company but his brother *bought* him *out* (= bought all his shares).

to cancel

The chairman said 'The expense of taking part in the trade fair should be *cancelled out* (= eliminated) by the increased number of orders we will receive.

to crowd, to pack

They didn't expect many people at the meeting but the hall was *crowded/packed out*.

to dry

After falling into the river the hunter built a fire to *dry* his clothes *out*.

to empty

When the little girl swallowed poison the doctors had to use a stomach pump to *empty* her stomach *out*.

to fall

Why is Anna crying? She had a bad dream and *fell out* of bed./ Ben and Bill have *fallen out* (= quarrelled) again.

to knock, to lay, to pass

The small boy swung his fist at the bully and with a lucky blow *knocked/laid him out* (= made him unconscious)./ Whenever I see a lot of blood I tend to *pass out* (= become unconscious).

to lose, to miss

Because the company put its tender in late it *lost/missed out* on the government contract./ The ice cream is nearly gone; if you don't hurry you'll *lose/miss out*.

to pan, to work

Harriet's marriage did not *pan/work out* very well; she's now divorced./ I've decided not to resign just yet but to wait and see how things *work out*.

to put

I *put* myself *out* (= inconvenienced myself) to help him and what thanks did I get?/ Can you post this letter for me? But don't put yourself out./ He was put out (= troubled) when his daughter moved away from home.

to speak

When others are speaking nonsense you must *speak out* (= say what you think).

to turn, to switch

The sky clouded over in the morning but the afternoon *turned out* to be fine./ Patricia is broken-hearted; it *turns out* that Joe doesn't want to marry her after all./ What have you got in your pockets?

Turn them *out* and let me see./ She was so annoyed she *turned* him *out* of the flat./ *Turn/switch out* the lights. (only used of lights and artificial fires. For all other electrical equipment and machines, the particle **off** is used.)

Exercises

1 *Complete these sentences by using phrasal verbs from those discussed above.*

1 Pilots who put their planes into sudden, steep dives often . . . . . . for a few seconds as a result of the terrible acceleration.
2 I tried to get some tickets for the new production of *Macbeth* last night but it was . . . .
3 I was going to bake a cake this morning but I found that I . . . . . . of flour.
4 We couldn't see a thing in the heavy fog; everything was . . . .
5 I wouldn't go anywhere in that ancient, rattletrap car of yours; it's likely to . . . . . . at any minute.
6 'What happened to Bill's scheme of emigrating to Australia?' 'Well, like all Bill's schemes it just . . . . . . and we heard no more about it.'
7 The grocer had a thriving business and several people tried to . . . . . . him . . . . . . but he refused to sell.
8 The painter had . . . . . . on the wall the dimensions of the mural he was going to paint.
9 The teacher said, 'My boy, I see that you have some very mistaken ideas of what is expected of you in this school. I'll have to . . . . . . you . . . .'
10 The government said that the new pension scheme was working well. There were only a few minor difficulties which could easily be . . . .
11 'What was the football match like?' 'Oh, it was . . . . There were so many people there that you could hardly move an inch.'
12 The committee expects our plans for the future development of the club in a week. We'll have to have an emergency meeting, sit down and . . . . . . something . . . .
13 If you want to measure a distance roughly you can always . . . . . . it . . . . One pace equals approximately one yard.
14 You messed your car up when you hit that tree, Joe. It'll cost you a bit to get those dents . . . .

15 Joe has planned everything in detail for the next five years. He's got it all . . . . . .

2 *Here is a list of pairs of phrasal verbs that are near opposites. Use one pair to complete each sentence below. (Make sure the verbs are in the right form).*

to tighten up/to loosen up; to put up/to tear down; to set off/to finish up; to live it up/to settle down; to drop off/to wake up; to slow down/ to speed up; to opt out/to join in; to be away/to be back; to wind up/to run down; to cross out/to write in.

1 We . . . . . to drive up to Scotland but, because the car broke down, we . . . . . by spending two days in a hotel about 50 miles out of London.
2 I went to see Mr. Smith yesterday but his secretary said that he . . . . . . in the Middle East and wouldn't . . . . . . until the end of the month.
3 When he was young he believed in enjoying himself so he . . . . . . a lot in many parts of the world but by the time he was fifty he had . . . . . . in a small village in the south of England.
4 You've let that clock . . . . . . again. I told you to . . . . . . it . . . . . . every Saturday.
5 The driving instructor said, 'You'll have to . . . . . . as you go through this village but when you see the 'end of the speed limit' sign you can . . . . . . again.
6 When we formed the syndicate to do the football pools Martin said that he wanted to . . . . . . but now, because we've won nothing, he has . . . .
7 Large cities are all the same. In some places large new buildings are being . . . . . . and in others old buildings are being . . . .
8 My grandmother loves television. The trouble is that she tends to . . . . . . half-way through a programme and then, when she . . . . . . she gets angry because she's missed it.
9 During the war the requirements for entry into the armed forces were . . . . . . a great deal but when the war was over they were . . . . . . again.
10 I'm not coming on that trip to Paris now so on your list you can . . . . . . my name . . . . . . but . . . . . . Janet's name . . . . . . because she's taking my place.

3 *Try to answer these questions using phrasal verbs from the above section and any other phrasal verbs that you can.*

1 What would happen if the main fuse on your house's electric switchboard suddenly blew?
2 'Did you go to the football match last week?'
   'Yes, I did but I didn't enjoy it.'
   'Why, what was the matter?'
3 Why is the winter in Europe a bad time for air traffic?
4 Why couldn't you get in to see the new play last night?
5 What do you usually do before you go to sleep if you've been reading in bed?
6 Why is a new ship or plane given severe tests before it's put into service?
7 The workers in the big factory wanted to play volley-ball at lunch-time, so what did they do?
8 What do big companies often do to little companies?
9 What happened to Jim's scheme of getting all the staff together for a Christmas celebration?
10 Why didn't you bake that cake you said you were going to bake this morning?

4 *Choose the correct verb from those given in brackets.*

1 Jack is not very good at telling lies. He usually gets (smooth/got/blown/caught/straightened) out when he doesn't tell the truth.
2 The moa, the giant bird of New Zealand, had (emptied/died/pulled/blown/drowned) out even before the Maoris came to that country.
3 In that box there's a mixture of French and Dutch stamps. Will you (cancel/spell/find/measure/sort) them out into two groups for me, please?
4 The platoon holding the hill had to retreat because they had (emptied/sold/conked/run/fizzled) out of ammunition.
5 'Did Bill get that job?'
   'No, he said he (cancelled/sold/missed/pulled/passed) out because he went for the interview on the wrong day.'
6 'What are those people waiting for over there? Go and see if you can (find/catch/sort/smell/pan) out.'
7 I can't control the car. My front right-hand tyre has (died/blown/emptied/lost/flattened) out!
8 The minister said, 'The agreement between our two countries has

certain problems but these are minor things that can easily be (beaten/hammered/flattened/panned/ironed) out.'

9 The new minister said, 'I intend to (cancel/stub/stamp/hammer/ sort) out corruption among government officials.'

10 Scientists often put forward theories which are later (borne/caught/ panned/blacked/drowned) out by other scientists' experiments.

11 'What happened at the meeting yesterday?'
 'Well, when it began it was rather stormy but everything (found/ got/sorted/worked/emptied) out all right.'

12 I didn't hear the football score on the radio today; it was (blown/ lost/drowned/stamped/beaten) out by a burst of static.

5 *In the following passages, provide either a suitable verb or a suitable particle. Discuss any alternatives.*

1 'Miss Jones, what's . . . . . . with you today? You've messed . . . . . . the report I gave you to type. Parts of it I can't . . . . . . out at all. And now you've . . . . . . up two of my appointments. And look, those invitations I asked you to . . . . . . out yesterday are still lying . . . . . . on your desk which, I must say, is rather more cluttered . . . . . . than usual.'
 'I'm sorry, Mr Grey but I'm feeling . . . . . . out this morning. I worked late last night and didn't finish until about 9 p.m. If you don't believe me the office cleaner will . . . . . . me out. And then I had to come . . . . . . at 7 this morning to type that report. I always do my best to . . . . . . out your instructions, Mr. Grey.'
 'I do apologize, Miss Jones. I forgot about that. Well, what can I do to . . . . . . up for my bad temper? I'll tell you what; you and I will . . . . . . out tonight at the best restaurant in town. I'll call for you at 8 o'clock.'
 'Oh, you are kind, Mr. Grey.'

2 'Oh, John, the drain outside the kitchen is . . . . . . up again. You'll have to clean it . . . . . . before you go to golf.'
 'But dear, the others will be teeing . . . . . . in a half an hour. If I don't go now I'll be late.'
 'Oh John I can't . . . . . . you out. Golf! That's all you think . . . . . . You can hardly wait to get . . . . . . every Sunday morning. I'm getting rather . . . . . . up with you and your golf. You let all these houschold jobs pile . . . . . . and when you come home during the week you say you're . . . . . . out. But you can always rake . . . . . . enough strength for golf on a Sunday. I used to be married to you but I've turned . . . . . . to be a golf widow!'

'But dear, if I don't get . . . . . . now I'll . . . . . . up the game for the others.'
'Oh belt . . . . . . then, and get . . . .'

6 *In the following sentences replace the italicized word or words by a suitable phrasal verb. Discuss any loss or gain in brevity, formality, emphasis, clarity.*

1 Will you *ascertain* for me how I can get from London to Tokyo by plane?
2 'I think my instructions are easy to understand but just to avoid any misunderstanding, I'll *say them very carefully and clearly* to you.'
3 I've been working on this algebra problem for hours but I can't *find the solution to it.*
4 I tried to get in to see the Cup Final last week but when I got to the stadium it was *so full of people that I couldn't get in.*
5 A few years ago in the USA there was an electrical fault which *caused* large areas of the country *to be completely without illumination.*
6 The speaker's words were *rendered inaudible* by the shouts of protesters in the crowd.
7 'Joe, my car's broken down again. If you help me to repair it that will *relieve you of the obligation to pay back* that £10 loan I gave you last week.'
8 The men got some wet sacks and *extinguished* the small grass fire *by beating it with them.*
9 The dinosaurs are something of a mystery; no one really knows why they suddenly *ceased to exist.*
10 Diplomacy is largely concerned with *finding suitable solutions to* problems and differences of opinion between nations.
11 At first the youth club had lots of activities for its members but through lack of leadership these *gradually became fewer and eventually ceased* and everyone lost interest.

7 *Try to answer these questions using phrasal verbs with* **out** *in the completive sense and any other phrasal verbs that you can.*
Work in pairs.

1 Why are you looking so worried over that arithmetic problem?
2 What is the danger of trying to cheat in an examination?
3 What happened to all those gigantic animals whose bones we see in Natural History museums?

4 What should you do with your cigarette when you have finished with it?

5 What is one of the functions of a police force?

6 These files in the filing cabinet are all mixed up; what shall I do with them?

7 Has that play been successful?

8 When a soldier is given an order what does he have to do?

9 Why didn't you stay at the Grand Hotel?

10 'It's forbidden to stop on the motorway.' 'Why has that car stopped then?'

16 Further uses of the particle *out*

Verbs used with *out* in the continuative-completive sense

Out used in this way conveys the sense of an action that is continued until some conclusion is reached.

e.g. The concert was boring but I sat it out for my wife's sake. (= I continued to sit there until the concert was finished)

a to bluff, to brazen, to face

The bank manager said to the clerk, 'Come on now, we know you stole the money. Own up. There's no use in trying to *bluff* it *out* (continue to deceive)./ I knew they knew I'd stolen the ring but I continued to *brazen* it *out* and they couldn't prove anything./ After the scandal they tried to make him resign but he decided to *face* it *out*.

b to have, to reason, to talk, to thrash, to think

Cecily hasn't spoken to Jack for two weeks so he's going to *have* it *out* with her (find out what's wrong)./ Let's not argue it about this matter; let's just *reason* it *out*./ The diplomat said, 'There are problems, but we must get to the conference table and *talk* them *out*./ Barbara was going to resign from her teaching job and break her contract, but I *talked* her *out* of it./ We must get together and *thrash* this whole problem *out* (= talk until a solution is reached)./ I'm confused; I'll have to sit down and *think* things *out*.

c to hold, to last, to ride, to see

I'm spending four weeks in the USA; I hope my money *holds out* (= lasts)./ The enemy *held out* (= persisted) for months before surrendering./ The strikers *held out* for a 20 per cent rise in wages./ The work on the farm was too hard and Joe didn't even *last* the week *out*./ Many of the marathon runners were tiring and it looked as though only about half would *last out* the distance./ The small ship managed to *ride out* the hurricane (= it didn't capsize)./ One of the film's directors was involved in a financial scandal but he *rode* it *out* (= survived)./ I won't agree to do the work for you unless I'm sure I can *see* it *out* (= finish it).

d to ferret, to fight, to hear, to hide, to shoot, to wear, to work

The information you want is somewhere in our files if you care to *ferret/winkle* it *out*./ Only one of you can come with me you'll have to *fight* it *out* among yourselves./ Some of the listeners interrupted but the speaker said, 'Wait, please *hear* me *out*.'/ After the bank robbery the thieves *hid out* for several weeks in an abandoned farmhouse./ The bandits *shot* it *out* with the police and two were killed./ I'll have to buy Billy a new pair of trousers; he *wears* his clothes *out* so quickly, the last pair are in holes./ The labourer said to the foreman, 'I want to leave the job but I'll *work* this week *out*.'

Out used in the initiative sense

Verbs used with **out** in this sense convey the idea of something beginning.

e to set, to start (compare **set off, start off**)

When the expedition *set/started out* there were high hopes that it would reach the summit of Mount Everest.

Out used in the instantaneous sense

This conveys the idea of something occurring suddenly. The particle is usually with a verb that conveys the idea of noise or making a noise.

f to bawl, to blurt, to burst, to call, to cry, to scream, to screech, to sing

The sergeant *bawled out* an order./ Without thinking, he *blurted out* all he knew about the murder./ When he saw me he *called out* my name./ The child *cried out* with pain./ The woman *screamed out* a warning as the child was about to run in to the busy road./ The old witch doctor *screeched out* a curse against his enemy./ When the teenagers saw the pop star arriving someone *sang/called/screamed out*, 'Here he comes!'.

g to blare, to chime (bells, clocks), **to peal** (bells), **to ring**

My neighbour's radio *blares out* at 6 o'clock every morning./ The grandfather clock *chimed out* the hours./ The church bells *pealed out* into the silent night./ A poem of Tennyson's begins '*Ring out* wild bells . . .'/ The horse's iron-shod hooves *rang out* against the cobblestones.

h to break, to burst

A fire *broke out* in the ship's hold./ Sweat *broke out* on his forehead./ He *broke out* in a rash./ War has *broken out*./ Rioting has *broken out* in several cities./ When the clown fell over the children *burst out* laughing./ When he heard screaming in the street, he *burst out* of the house to see what was happening.

Exercises

1 *In each space in the passages below put either a suitable verb from those discussed above, and earlier, or a suitable particle. (Make sure the verbs are in the correct form).*

1 The defenders of the village held . . . . . . for many weeks but in the end they gave . . . . . . because their food and water had run . . . . The enemy commander was surprised they had . . . . . . out so long but after . . . . . . out a few stubborn resisters who had . . . . . . out in cellars and attics, he was able to carry . . . . . . the rest of his plan.

2 The speaker in Hyde Park said as the crowd began to drift . . . . . . 'Don't go . . . . . . Listen! The message I bring has come . . . . . . from the stars, from my masters in Alpha Centauri. I must carry . . . . . . their instructions to save the world. All of us have been sold . . . . . . by racketeers and capitalists. If we don't act now, it's all . . . . . . with us; we'll all be wiped . . . . . . by greed and corruption. Mark my words, this will all turn . . . . . . to be true. Now is the time to . . . . . . it out with them.' He got no further because he was shouted . . . . . . by a section of the crowd.

3 'How's the job going, Joe?'

'Oh, not so good. I'm really a bit fed . . . . . . with it.'

'Why, what's . . . . . . ? You're holding . . . . . . a good job and you say you're fed . . . .'

'I wouldn't say it's all that good. I should have . . . . . . out for something better but this looked good at the time and I thought that things would . . . . . . out all right.'

'But they haven't then?'

'Not really. Look, here I am cooped . . . . . . in this tiny office all day and all I do is carry . . . . . . other people's instructions. I'm never allowed to make . . . . . . my own mind about anything. The work just piles . . . . . . in my in-tray and when I knock . . . . . . at night I'm . . . . . . out. It all boils . . . . . . to the fact that I'm no more than a petty clerk. I doubt whether I'll . . . . . . out another week the way I feel now.'

'What you want, Joe, is to relax a bit. Why don't you and I go . . . . . . tonight? We could eat . . . . . . at a Chinese restaurant and perhaps wind . . . . . . at a night club. Let's live it . . . . . . a bit for a change.'

'Good idea! Count me . . . .'

2 *Choose the correct verb from those given in brackets.*

1 The people who campaigned against slavery (worked/held/helped/fought it/thrashed it) out against all opposition and won in the end.

2 Jane has just left school but she knows what she's going to do in the future; she has (held/counted/ferreted/worn/thought) it all out.

3 I'm glad when the week-end comes. By Friday I always feel (fought/worked/worn/shot/counted) out.

4 Susan is a hard person to get to know properly. I went to school with her but sometimes even I can't (reason/work/winkle/fathom/see) her out.

5 That philosophy course is so boring that I don't think I'll (wear/last/ride/brave/count it out.

6 The boy who was trying to get into the football match without a ticket asked his friend what he should do if someone asked him for it. His friend said, 'Say anything, say you've lost it, just (fight/brazen/see/reason/hide) it out.'

3 *Put* **off, out, in** *or* **up** *in each of the spaces overleaf.*

1 'Why are you looking so happy?' 'Tomorrow morning I'm . . . . . . to the Costa Brava for two weeks' holiday.'
2 'Don't go home yet; it's still early.' 'No, I'm . . . . . . It's late enough for me and tomorrow's a working day.'
3 Everything's getting more expensive. I see by the paper that petrol's . . . . . . again.
4 We have a saying in English, 'The balloon's going . . . . . .' which means that something is about to happen.'
5 Mr. Smith is not . . . . . . ; he's . . . . . . to lunch. He'll be back at 2 p.m.
6 Barbara is an early riser. She's usually . . . . . . at about 6 every morning.
7 You look very unhappy this morning. What's . . . . . . with you?
8 I'm . . . . . . of writing paper. Lend me a few sheets please.
9 When the plane had to make an emergency landing in fog Jane really thought it was all . . . . . . with her.
10 'Let's pass the hat round and collect some money for a wedding present for the boss.' 'Right! I'm . . . . . . Here's a pound.'
11 Mary asked for the 'soup of the day' but the waiter told her it was . . . .
12 'How's Jane doing in the golf tournament this year?'
   'She's doing well. She's still . . . . . . and with a bit of luck she might pull it . . . .'

4 *Replace the italicized word or words in each sentence below with a suitable phrasal verb with* **out**. *Discuss any loss or gain in brevity, formality or emphasis.*

1 Although the student knew that his cheating in the examination had been discovered he decided to *continue to act as though he were innocent.*
2 Bill got a job in the Middle East but from the tone of his letters I don't think that he will *continue to work there until his contract expires.*
3 The weather report said that, although the storm was severe it would *continue in this way and then cease* after several hours.
4 The office staff could not decide who was to make the speech at the annual dinner party so I left them to *continue the argument* among themselves *until they came to a decision.*
5 The speaker said, 'The police must *eradicate* this terrible crime of mugging elderly people in the streets.'
6 When the company came under new ownership there was a great

deal of adjustment of staff and Marie, who was unhappy and angry, finally decided *to talk about all the problems* with her boss.

7 The student had this problem of how to study and how to earn enough money to support himself at the same time. His friend told him that he would sit down with him and *attack it logically until they found a solution.*

8 The boxer was knocked down and was *unable to get up before the referee had counted to ten.*

5 *Look again at the use of:* **off, down, out** *with the verb* **die.** *When you have done this put the appropriate particle in each space below.*

1 The Australian Aborigines used to have elaborate initiation ceremonies but today these old customs are dying . . . .

2 The protesters who had thrown smoke bombs into the embassy building waited until the commotion and panic had died . . . . . . and then mixed with the crowds.

3 The World Wildlife Fund was started to try to save certain species which are in danger of dying . . . .

4 When I came back from my summer holidays I found that my potplants had died . . . .

5 The yachts stayed in harbour until the storm had died . . . .

6 Rumours rise and spread very swiftly but they die . . . . . . just as quickly.

6 *Try to answer these questions using phrasal verbs with the* **out** *from those discussed above, and any other phrasal verbs that you can. Discuss any alternatives. Work in pairs.*

1 How do you feel if you do too much exercise in one day?

2 If you have a problem, what is the best thing to do?

3 Why do nations often have conferences?

4 If you are the sort of person who never gives up, and you think that someone in your firm is trying to keep an important plan secret from you, what would you do?

5 What did the bank robbers do when their hide-out was surrounded by armed police?

6 If someone has some information that he is unwilling to part with, what do you have to do if you really want it?

17 Uses of the particle *over*

This particle can be used with certain verbs in the continuative-completive sense. With these verbs the idea is conveyed of an action that is continuing with the aim of reaching some conclusion e.g. a decision.

a to chew, to mull, to thin, to turn, to talk

It's a difficult decision to make. You'll have to give me time to *think* it *over*./ Don't sign the contract yet. *Chew/mull* it *over* for a few days./ When I asked him a question about his past life, I could see he was *turning* it *over* in his mind./ 'Are you going to buy a new car?' 'I must *talk* it *over* with my wife first.'

b With some verbs, **over** conveys the idea of transfer.

to take, to hand, to sign, to make, to get, to put, to across

The ship has been sold. The new owners *take over* tomorrow./ The captain of the plane said to his co-pilot, 'I'll *take over* now.'/ The thief said, 'Come on, *hand over* your wallet'./ The man told his son 'I intend to *sign/make over* all my shares in the company over to you./ Joe is a bore at parties. He insists on telling jokes but he can't *get* them *over*.

c With some verbs, **over** conveys completive sense, usually of leaving something unpleasant behind.

to be, to have, to get, to blow, to pass

I had my final exam yesterday; it's good to *get/have* it *over* (with) The woman said to the dentist 'Start now and let's *get* it *over* with as soon as we can./ The storm will soon *blow/pass over*. The MP was in the centre of a political scandal but it soon *passed/blew over*.

With other verbs **over** is used in the completive sense to convey the idea of completely covering the surface of something.

to cloud, to cover, to freeze, to frost, to ice, to mist

The sky has *clouded over*; it's g;oing to rain./ The surface of the bookcase was *covered over* with a thin layer of dust./ The lake has *iced/frozen over*./ On rainy days it is sometimes difficult to see through the car window because they *mist over*.

d The particle **over** is often used in the sense of falling from an upright vertical position or to lean from this position.

Sometimes there is very little distinction between the use of **over** and **down** in this context. However, **over** is more often used of people, boats, vehicles, and when referring to smaller standing objects e.g. vases, chairs, small trees.

The main verbs used with **over** are:

to blow, to bowl, to fall, to lean, to heel, to lie, to keel, to knock, to kick, to push, to shove, to topple, to trip

As I was going in, a man came running out of the building and almost *bowled* me *over*./ The first time Joe saw Jill, he was *bowled over (fig.)* and a month later they were married./ The news that I had won £1000 in the lottery *bowled* me *over*./ The toddler *fell over* and hit his head on the leg of a chair./ The vase of flowers *fell over*./ When the gust of wind hit the yacht, she *leaned/heeled/lay over*./ Barbara looked rather pale and then without warning she *keeled over*./ Be careful or you'll *knock over* your cup of coffee./ You could have *knocked* me *over* with a feather (*coll. phrase*) when I heard that Joe was married./ Billy, don't play on the road or you'll get *knocked over*./ The boy was angry when his brother *kicked* his bicycle *over* in a fit of temper./ An elephant can *push over* quite a large tree with its head./ Large lorries were *toppled over* in the terrible gale./ As I felt my way across the darkened room I stumbled against a chair and *tripped over*.

e **Over** can also convey the sense of too much or more than expected.

to be (left), to boil, to brim, to bubble, to carry, to have, to run, to spill, to stop

When the children had finished eating at the party there was very little *over/left over*./ After Mary had paid her rent and her bills there was very little money *over/left over.*/ Turn the heat down under that soup or it will *boil over.*/ After the heavy rains the rivers were *brimming over.*/ He filled the glass so full that it was *brimming over.*/ You left the tap on and the bath is *brimming/running over.*/ She was *bubbling over (fig.)* with happiness./ How much money did you *have over* after your holiday in Spain?/ The vase was heavy and some water *spilled over* as she carried it over to the windowsill./ There were so many people in the meeting that they *spilled over* into a neighbouring room./ On my way to Singapore I decided to *stay/stop over* for several days in Bangkok.

f With many verbs **over** is used to express repetition. It is generally, but not always, used with **again**. To emphasize continued repetition, **over and over** is often used. **All over again** therefore means 'to start again from the beginning'.

I made a mistake, I'll have to calculate that *over again.*/ *Read* your notes *over* before the examination./ I just want to *run over* these calculations./ He played the same record *over and over* (again). I've made a mistake, I'll have to start *all over again.*

g **Over** is often used with verbs of cleaning. It has a sense of hurried, careless, cleaning.

to brush, to rub, to sweep, to wipe

The carpet looks a little better; I *brushed* it *over* last night./ Don't worry too much about the table, just *rub* it *over* with a cloth./ We haven't much time but we'd better just *sweep over* the kitchen floor./ The car is not very clean; I only had time to *wipe* it *over* this morning.

Exercises

1 *Complete each sentence below by using an appropriate phrasal verb with* **over.**

1 When the large savage dog bounded towards him, the small boy was so frightened that he . . . . . . as he tried to run away.
2 Oh yes, it was love at first sight with Piers; he took one look at Amanda and was . . . . . .
3 Winter is almost here. The pools in the garden are . . . .
4 I hate going to see Alfred. Come on, let's go now and . . . . . . it . . . . . . with.

5 You can't expect me to make up my mind at once; I'll have to . . . . . . it . . . . . . for a few days.
6 I tried to explain to the government official what my problem was but I couldn't . . . . . . my message . . . .
7 Many ships were forced to stay in port until the hurricane had . . . .
8 The chairman said, 'Before we begin to discuss this subject again, let me just . . . . . . the points that were made at our last meeting.
9 Look at the mess on the cooker. Someone has let the porridge . . . .
10 She was very unhappy and her eyes . . . . . . with tears.
11 Jane messed up her history homework and she has to . . . . . . it . . . . . . again.
12 Miss Smith asked me to . . . . . . her class this morning as she had an appointment with the doctor.

2 *Complete the following passages by either filling each space with an appropriate phrasal verb or by choosing the correct word from those given in brackets. Discuss any alternatives.*

1 Fred has been holding (up/down/out/off/in) the job of acting manager for three months now. He seems to be getting rather (knocked/packed/fed/blown/set) up because he feels that he is being messed (down/off/out/over/about) too much. He hopes, however, that when the new owners . . . . . . all his troubles will also . . . .
2 Some students get very (keyed/blown/clogged/roughed/broken) up before an important examination. One friend of mine used to . . . . . . in a red rash all over his face and chest. When the examination . . . . . . , however, and his nerves had (died/broken/worn/calmed/narrowed) down, the rash just went (out/off/over/down/away).
3 When we . . . . . . from Manchester to drive down to London it was early winter and in some places the roads were . . . . I was nervous and every time Harry began to speed (off/away/up/out/around) I told him to (speed/stop/break/slow/pull) down. Because the windows were closed the glass kept on . . . . . . and this made me more nervous. Finally I saw a small roadside cafe and I told Harry to (stop/pull/break/close/wrap) up for a short time while I calmed (off/up/out/over/down).
4 'I read in the papers that your firm has been . . . . . . by a multinational. How secure is your job, then?'

'Well, I don't know yet but I've (done/fed/closed/worked/made) up my mind to (hold/stay/keep/see/wear) on here as long as I can. If I lose this job I'll only have to . . . . . again with some other firm. So, I'll just wait until the fuss and bother of the change-over . . . . . . and then see what happens.'

5 When the war . . . . . . many British ex-servicemen thought that they would like to (get/lie/pack/settle/sit) down and lead a quiet life. However, they soon (thought/found/panned/caught/bore) out that to be (hammered/glued/strapped/clamped/tied) down to one job was not what they wanted. The idea of starting work at 9 a.m. and knocking (out/off/down/over/about) at 5 p.m. did not appeal to all of them. So, some of them sold (out/up/away/down/over) everything they possessed, paid (off/out/down/over/in) all their debts and, with the money that was . . . . . . they . . . . . . to try their luck in some other country like Australia. For some it (carried/pulled/topped/paid/bought) off; for others it didn't.

3 *Use your dictionary to find out the difference in meaning between the two verbs in italics in the following sentences.*

I think Jane will be able *to get* her operation *over* before Christmas.
I think Jane will be able *to get over* her operation before Christmas.

When you have done that put one of these verbs in each space below. Don't forget you might need **it** as well.

1 The teacher is in a bad mood this morning but she'll soon
. . . .
2 My brother had a heart attack but he has . . . . fairly well.
3 If I have to go to the dentist I like to . . . . as quickly as possible.
4 My old aunt was disappointed in love when she was young and she never . . . .
5 Let's start the meeting now and try to . . . . before 12 o'clock.

4 *Replace the italicized word or words in each of the following sentences by a phrasal verb chosen from those discussed above. Discuss any loss or gain in brevity, formality, emphasis etc.*

1 The strong man *used his hands to make* the lion tamer *fall*.
2 Before I give you an answer to your question I'll have to *consider it at some length*.

3 The new teacher will *assume responsibility* for the class tomorrow.
4 We want this programme to run smoothly so that everything will *be concluded* by 11.30.
5 Unfortunately a lot of people had eaten before they came to the party, so a lot of food *remained*.
6 As the first three points on the agenda of the meeting took longer than expected, the last two points *were left to be dealt with at the next meeting*.

5 *Put one of these particles* — **up, down, out, over** — *in each space below*.

1 Alice has some good arguments to present to the committee. I only hope that she can put them . . . .
2 She threw a wet cloth over the blazing frying pan and managed to put the flames . . . .
3 I don't want that dog inside all night. Put him . . . . . . please.
4 Mary is feeling rather cut up this morning because she had to have her old dog put . . . . . . yesterday.
5 The newspapers criticized the petrol companies for putting . . . . . . petrol prices again.
6 The car company put . . . . . . a new handbook to help owners to maintain their own cars.
7 I've carried this heavy bag from the railway station; I'm glad to be able to put it . . . .
8 The stranger turned to me, said 'Hello' and put . . . . . . his hand for me to shake.

6 *Answer these questions using as many phrasal verbs as you can from those discussed above and any other phrasal verbs. Work in pairs.*

1 What is the best thing to do when you have done something badly?
2 What is the best thing to do when you have something unpleasant that you must do?
3 What might happen when you are cooking rice if you don't watch it carefully and turn the heat down?
4 If you were returning from Australia to London would you fly direct?
5 What is the wisest thing to do if you have a decision to make that will affect your future?
6 What is that noise I can hear?
7 What did the class do when the teacher told them a funny story?

8 What sort of news do we read in the papers every day?
9 What makes you think that it is going to rain?
10 If you are a journalist or broadcaster what is the most important thing that you have to do?

18 The use of *on* and *off* to convey attachment and detachment

With some verbs both particles can be used to form a pair of opposites.

a Verbs of hitting

to bash, to belt, to hammer, to hit, to knock

The mechanic *bashed/hit* the wheel *on/off*./ The heel came off her shoe and she *hammered* it *on* again with a stone./ The geologist *knocked off* a piece of rock with his hammer./ Joan and Mary *hit* it *off* (= are very friendly) very well, they share a flat.

b Verbs of forcing, pulling, pushing

to force, to get, to pull, to push, to slide, to slip

Don't *force* the lid *off/on*./ I *got* this belt *on* and now I can't *get* it *off*./ The boy *pulled* his trousers *on/off*./ She *pushed* him *on/off* the bus./ You have to slide the *covering on/off* carefully./ He *slipped* his clothes *off* and dived into the river.

Verbs used with off only

c Verbs of cutting, breaking

to break, to chip, to chop, to clip, to cut, to file, to hack, to plane, to saw, to scrape, to shave, to shoot, to slice, to snap, to snip, to strike, to tear

The girl *broke off* a piece of chocolate and gave it to her friend./ The sailors *chipped* the paint *off* with small hammers./ The butcher *chopped/cut/sliced off* a large piece of meat./ Leo *clipped/snipped off* the rough edge of paper with some sharp scissors./ That piece of wood is too long, *cut/plane/saw* a couple of inches *off*. The bolt is stuck, I shall have to *file* it *off*./ He didn't have a sharp knife, so he had to *hack off* a piece of bread with a blunt one./ This piece of wood is too big for the hole; I'll have to *scrape, shave/plane* a bit *off*./ It's broken; I leaned on it and the top *snapped off*./ The executioner *struck* the traitor's head *off* with one blow./ Don't fool about with that rifle or you'll *shoot/blow* your head *off*.

d Verbs of cleaning, washing etc.

to brush, to dust, to scrape

There's dandruff on your collar; *brush* it *off*./ He *dusted off* the pile of old books and began to look through them. You've spilled jam on the table cloth; now *scrape* it *off*.

e Verbs of division and separation

to block, to cordon, to curtain, to cut, to partition, to rail, to rope, to seal, to shut, to wall

The police *blocked off* the main road while the procession passed./ The police *cordoned off* the area where the robbers were hiding out./ Part of the room was *curtained/partitioned off* to make a sleeping area./ The patrol was *cut off* and couldn't return to base./ This is a small village and I feel very *cut off*./ I got on to Mary on the phone but I was *cut off* (= the line went dead)./ During the earthquake the electricity was *cut off*./ The dangerous part of the cliff path had been *railed/roped off*./ No one could enter the area where the explosion had occurred; it was *sealed off*./ The house was so large that the owner had *shut off* some of the rooms./ The swimming pool was *walled off* from the rest of the garden.

f Verbs of separation and division from the whole

to burn, to come, to cream, to fall, to measure, to take

The farmers *burnt off* the dead grass./ The door handle has *come/ fallen off* again./ I have a wonderful plan for developing the land but I'm not sure that it will *come off* (*fig.*, = succeed)./ The ministry decided to *cream off* (take the best) the best pupils from the various schools in the district and put them in a special college./ The number of applications for university places has *fallen off* (= diminished) this year./ The shop-keeper *measured off* two metres of cloth from the roll./ Take your hat off./ He's very amusing, and good at imitating people, he *takes off* (= mimics) the boss very well.

Verbs used with *on* only

g Verbs of attachment

to belt, to buckle, to clip, to fasten, to fit, to glue, to hook, to jam, to nail, to paste, to pin, to sew, to stick, to tie

The climber *belted/buckled/clipped* his harness *on./ Fasten/pin* this badge *on* for me./ Can you *fit* a new washer *on* to the spin dryer?/ I'll just *glue/paste/stick* the label *on./* Back the car in and I'll *hook* the trailer *on./* Someone has *jammed* this lid *on* and I can't get it off./ *Nail* that picture *on* to the wall./ I'll be ready in a minute, I've just got to *tie on* the rope.

h Other verbs

to catch, to latch, to tag

Catch on to this branch and I'll try to pull you out of the water./ I made signs to Joan to keep quiet about what we had discussed but she didn't *catch on* (= understand quickly) and blurted everything out./ No, I didn't enjoy the outing at all; Nicola *latched on* to me for the whole day./ Wherever Bill goes, his young brother *tags on.*

1 *In each space below put a suitable verb from those discussed earlier or a suitable particle.*

1 If I hadn't held my hat . . . . . . firmly, the wind would have . . . . . . it off.
2 My wife was born and lived in the city and in this small village, although she . . . . . . it off quite well with the villagers, she still feels . . . . . . off.
3 I told you not to . . . . . . the top of this container on. Now it's . . . . . . on tightly and I can't . . . . . . it off unless I . . . . . . it off which will probably break it.
4 That door handle shouldn't . . . . . . off again in a hurry; I've . . . . . . it on tightly.
5 Valerie hurried . . . . . . and said, 'I'm late and I have to go

. . . . . . again in a few minutes. I'll just have time to . . . . . . this dress off, ... on a fresh one, make my face . . . . . . a bit and then hurry . . . . . . again'.

6 Some fool must have . . . . . . this wheel on with a heavy hammer. It'll need a couple of strong men to . . . . . . it off.

7 At the conference, name labels were handed . . . . . . to all the participants and they were asked to . . . . . . them on to their coats.

8 I . . . . . . the stew on at 2 o'clock and a half an hour later Barbara turned . . . . . . and wanted to chat so that I forgot to turn the heat . . . . . . and the whole thing boiled . . . . . . ; I really messed . . . . . . my nice clean cooker.

9 'This nut has been . . . . . . on so tightly that I'll have to use a heavy spanner to . . . . . . it off. If that won't do it I'll have to use a hacksaw and . . . . . . it off.'

10 A button has . . . . . . off your shirt. You'd better . . . . . . it on again before you lose it.

11 Although I spell my instructions . . . . . . for Bill he just doesn't seem to . . . . . . on.

12 I . . . . . . the heel of my shoe off this morning. If I can get some strong glue I can . . . . . . it on so that it won't . . . . . . off again.

13 If that chap Jones looks at me at a party I always look . . . . . . because if you give him any encouragement, he will come . . . . . . and . . . . . . on to you for the rest of the night.

14 George is all dressed . . . . . . in his best suit tonight. I wonder why he . . . . . . that on. Perhaps he was expecting to see Emma here but she hasn't turned . . . .

15 The farmers were . . . . . . off the dry rice stalks left after the harvest when a fire broke . . . . . . in some nearby trees. It could have been dangerous but they managed to beat it . . . . . . fairly quickly.

2 *Look again at the use of* **out, up, off**, *with the verb* **to measure**. *When you have done this, put one of these particles in each space below.*

1 The carpenter who is going to build the new shelves in the kitchen is coming to day to measure . . . .

2 When the explorers were crossing the desert each person's share of water was measured . . . . . . carefully each day.

3 Cooks often use cups, glasses and spoons to measure . . . . . . the ingredients for their dishes.

4 Sue started her new job today. It's fairly difficult but I'm sure that she'll measure . . . . . . to it.
5 Measure . . . . . . two yards from that coil of rope please.
6 That board is exactly two metres long. Now I want you to measure . . . . . . exactly 55 cm. from one end.

3 *In each space below put* **out, up, off** *or* **down**.

1 That radio's too loud; you can listen to it but please turn it . . . .
2 Turn the cooker . . . . . . ; the stew will be cooked now.
3 Did many people turn . . . . . . at the concert last night?
4 I can't hear the music; turn the volume . . . . . . a bit please.
5 John applied to join that exclusive club but he was turned . . . . . .
6 'What happened to that friend of Sue's who, she said, was an under secretary?'
'Oh him! He turned . . . . . . to be nothing but a low grade civil servant.'

4 *Answer these questions using as many phrasal verbs as you can from those discussed above and any other phrasal verbs. Work in pairs.*

1 Why did you have so much trouble in unscrewing that nut?
2 What are some of the disadvantages of living in a small town?
3 Why can't you open the door?
4 I heard that John injured himself when he went shooting yesterday. What happened?
5 What did Ian do when he saw the child struggling in the river?
6 'How's business this year, Richard? A lot of nice profits?'
7 This piece of wood is too long and too thick. What shall I do?
8 Why isn't the refrigerator going?
9 The lid of this little ivory box is very fragile. How can I get it on without breaking it?
10 King Charles I of England was executed, wasn't he? What did they do to him?

5 *Complete these sentences using a phrasal verb or an appropriate particle. Discuss any alternatives.*

1 The old building was in danger of falling down so the authorities . . . . . . the area . . . .

2 The workmen . . . . . . the part of the road that had subsided and they put . . . . . . a sign warning motorists to slow . . . .

3 You had better nail that lid . . . . . . or the box may come open on the journey. We don't want the books to . . . .

4 The family were cooped . . . . . . in one tiny room and they had . . . . . . one end as a sleeping area.

5 During the war many cities were almost wiped . . . . . . and it is a wonder that anyone ever . . . . . . out of the horrors alive.

6 When I try to give Barbara advice she just won't listen. She seems to . . . . . . part of her mind sometimes so that you just can't . . . . . . your message . . . . . . to her.

7 It was difficult for her but she was so determined that she never gave . . . . . . trying and the gamble came . . . . . . in the end.

8 British governments have a reputation for messing . . . . . . the economy but, despite this, they seem to manage so that in the end everything . . . . . . out all right.

19 The use of *on* to express the continuative aspect of the verb

On is commonly used to express the continuing action of a verb. For emphasis the particle is often repeated — **on and on**. It may also convey a sense of continuing further along or further in.

a In this sense **on** is often used with verbs of motion. Examples are

to come, to go, to hurry, to march, to move, to run, to struggle, to walk

With some verbs of motion, **on** can be combined with other directional particles. Some verbs of motion are sometimes used figuratively with an extended meaning.

Come *on up*. You *go on in*; I'll wait here./ I can't understand what she is *going on* (= making a fuss) about./ She *hurried on*, afraid she was going to be late./ Hurry *on down*!/ The army *marched on and on* into the mountains./ It's time we *moved on*./ He *ran on* steadily, even though it was pouring with rain./ The explorers' water had run out but they *struggled on*./ *Walk on*, I'll catch up with you in a minute.

b Another group of verbs convey the idea of continuance, or endurance.

to carry, to get, to go, to keep, to press, to push, to soldier

When the headmaster entered the room he said to the class 'Don't stop. *Carry/get/keep on* with your work.'/ The workers *carried/went/kept on* despite the weather./ I hear that John is *carrying on* (= behaving in a way of which people disapprove) with someone else' wife./ I can't understand why young people today *carry/go on* the way they do./ I admit I made a mistake but there's no need to *go/*

113

keep on (= make a fuss) about it./ The scientist searching for the new vaccine *pressed/pushed on* with his work night and day./ 'How is Mary's business going?' 'Not too well but she is *soldiering* on.' (= continuing determinedly despite difficulties)

c to draw, to drag, to wear
These verbs suggest a slow and weary progression

It's getting colder; winter is *drawing on*. (= approaching slowly, this is usually used of seasons)/ As the long summer's day *dragged/wore on*, most of the children were half asleep.

d to be, to come, to fight, to play, to read, to sleep, to study, to work

What's on at the Odeon tonight?/ I have a cold *coming on* (= developing)./ Your golf is *coming on* (= improving)./ Will you *come on* or we'll miss the train!/ Although the war was over, some soldiers in isolated places *fought on*./ An old song says 'Casey he waltzed with his strawberry blonde while the band *played on*!'/ The student *read/studied on* far into the night./ Despite the noise the tired child *slept on*./ You can knock off if you like but I am going to *work on*.

e to hang, to hold, to stay, to stop

These verbs suggest maintaining a position.

Don't be in such a hurry, just *hang/hold on* will you?/ 'Mr Smith on the phone for you.' 'Ask him to *hang/hold on* for a minute will you?'/ You can go home; I think I'll *stay/stop on* for a while./ John like Amsterdam so much that he *stayed/stopped on* for another week.

Exercises

1 *In each space in the passages below put either a suitable verb or a suitable particle. Discuss any alternatives.*

  1 The soldier said, 'I'm fed . . . . . with this war. It just seems to . . . . . . on and on. When it's all . . . . . . I'm going to get married, set . . . . . . house in a small village somewhere and settle . . . . If I can only . . . . . . on until the war ends I can do it because I've saved . . . . . quite a bit of money from my pay which I can . . . . . . back on.'

114

2 The way that husband of Joan's . . . . . . on at parties is a disgrace. He drinks too much and then he latches . . . . . . to people and starts to . . . . . . on about his experiences abroad. He usually get so carried . . . . . by the sound of his own voice that he . . . . . . on and on even when most of his audience have drifted . . . . . . It's time someone told him to belt . . . .

3 'Don't wait out there. . . . . . . on in. Mary's upstairs. She'll be . . . . . . in a moment. Where are you two . . . . . . to tonight?'
'Well, we thought we might go to the Odeon. There's a new film . . . . . . there tonight. I wish Mary would hurry . . . . . . Time's . . . . . . on and if we don't get there early we're likely to find the place packed . . . .'

4 I'm thinking of setting myself . . . . . . in business. How do you think I'd . . . . . . on if I went . . . . . . to the bank and asked for a loan? Would they . . . . . . me out?'
'I don't see why they should. You've been holding . . . . . . a good job for some years now and you must have a bit of money put . . . .'
'Yes, I suppose I should talk it . . . . . . with the bank manager. After all I'm a customer and it's his job to help his customers, isn't it?'
'Of course. They put . . . . . . all those pamphlets saying, 'Come . . . . . . and talk . . . . . . your money problems with us. We are patient. We'll listen and so on. So, don't . . . . . . back any longer. Get . . . . . . to the bank and get it . . . . . . with.'

5 The foreman said to the workers, ' . . . . . . on you blokes, there's work to do, so let's . . . . . . on with it. We're not paid to laze . . . . . . and smoke the time . . . . First let's clean . . . . . . this storeroom. Joe, you can sweep . . . . . . Clear . . . . . . all that straw and packing paper that's lying . . . . . . And Fred, you can . . . . . . on with what you were doing yesterday. Those small packages have to be crated . . . . . . and make sure they're nailed . . . . . . properly. There are two different sorts of packages so don't muddle them . . . . Half have to be shipped . . . . . . to the Middle East and the others to Nigeria. Oh, now I'm not quite sure about that. . . . . . . on a minute and I'll go and check . . . . . . at the office.'
'Right,' said Fred, 'I suppose I can . . . . . . on with smoking my cigarette then.'

2 *Complete each sentence with a suitable phrasal verb with* **on**.

1 'I won't be long. Can you . . . . . . a minute?'
2 I thought the lecture was never going to stop. It just . . . .
3 'How are you . . . . . . in your new house?'
  'Oh, fine, thank you.'
4 Shall we knock off now or shall we . . . . . . for a little longer?
5 'I'm tired. Let's rest here for a while.'
  'No, we had better . . . . . . because it'll be dark soon.'
6 My nose and head feel all stuffed up. I think I've got a cold . . . .
7 Life's certainly hard at times but we just have to . . . .
8 That young son of Janet's is very badly behaved. The way he . . . . . . in front of other people is disgraceful.
9 The headmaster heard the noise in the classroom, walked in and said, 'Now, just what's . . . . . . in here?'

3 *Answer these questions using phrasal verbs from those discussed above and any other phrasal verbs that you can. Work in pairs.*

1 Do you go to the cinema often?
2 Why are you leaving the party so early?
3 I see that your company has been taken over by the Americans. What are you going to do now?
4 How did George get on when he went along to the bank and asked for a loan to buy a new car?
5 Why are you still working? It's late!
6 Why did you leave the lecture early?
7 Can you tell me what happened when you went walking in the country yesterday?

20 The uses of the particle *through*

a Through is used with certain verbs in a completive sense.

to be, to break, to get, to pull

I'll *be through* (= finished) at 6 p.m./ I've tried to help Rebecca but it's no good; *I'm through* with her./ When you*'re through* with that book I'll have it./ I tried to ring you but I couldn't *get through* (= establish communication)./ Brian's a strange fellow; I try to talk to him but I can't *get through*./ I've a lot of work to *get through* (= complete)./ John is having his medical test for the army today but I don't think he'll *get through* (= pass). The streets were so crowded that we couldn't *get through* to the town hall. The doctors seeking a cure for cancer are confident that they will *break through* (= suddenly find the solution) one day./ My father was very ill last year but he *pulled through* (= survived). Can you see the double meaning of this verb in the joke 'the wounded man was at death's door and the doctors *pulled* him *through*.'?

b Through is also used with verbs in the continuative-completive sense.

to follow, to live, to look, to muddle, to play, to read, to run, to see, to sit, to win

When she starts a job, she always *follows* it *through* (= completes it)./ After you have hit the golf ball your swing must *follow through*./ It is a miracle that anyone *lived through* the terrible earthquake./ I've looked through the list but my name isn't on it./ The British have a reputation of being able to *muddle through* (= succeed more by accident than by design). Fred's business affairs are in a bad way but I suppose he'll *muddle through* as usual./ 'Today,' the conductor

117

said, 'We'll *play* the concerto right *through.'*/ *Read* these notes *through* before the meeting./ Would you like to *run through* the programme with me again?/ I have enough money to *see* me *through.*/ I had to *see* that boring foreign movie *through* again last night./ Don't worry about your application to join the club; I'll *see* it *through* (= guide it through)./ Do we have to *sit through* that tedious graduation ceremony again this year?/ Margaret is having difficulties with her studies now, but she'll *win through* (= succeed in the end).

1 *Complete each of the following sentences by using either* **off, out, over, through, about** *or* **around.**

1 This lid is jammed on and I can't get it . . . .
2 I hear that the car company are getting . . . . . . a new model this year.
3 There is a story going . . . . . . that the P.M. is going to resign.
4 Let's go and sign the agreement. I like to get these matters . . . . . . with.
5 'Have Alex and Lydia gone on holiday yet?'
   'Yes, they finally got . . . . . . at about 6 this morning.'
6 Laura had a row with Paul last night. She told him to get . . . . . . and never come back.
7 Before he entered the deserted building, the detective got . . . . . . his pistol.
8 Jonathan has never got . . . . . . his wife's death in that car accident.
9 Barbara's a nice girl but I don't think she's very bright. I just can't get . . . . . . to her.
10 'Did you manage to ring New York?'
   'Yes, I got . . . . . . at midnight.'
11 My father was very active as a young man but he doesn't get . . . . . . very much now.

2 *Choose the correct phrasal verb from those given in brackets.*

1 It's a soldier's duty to (bring off/carry out/put across/see through) the orders of his superiors.
2 'Why are you limping, John?'
   'Oh, that old wound of mine is (bottling up/grinding down/breaking down/playing up) again.'

118

3 The negotiations between the two countries concerning the border dispute (wore out/ran through/broke down/messed up).

4 No one seems interested in playing football on Saturday so let's (call off/get over/black out/switch off) the game.

5 Jenny and Nicky could never share a flat because they don't (put it across/carry it out/hit it off/see it through).

6 Sylvia said that a big multi-national is trying to (take over/sell out/win through/pay off) the company she works for.

7 After the meeting the company director said, 'Well, I think we've just about got that deal with James & Co. (boiled down/sewn up/counted in/worn out).'

8 Mark sold up all his property and went to Australia but it didn't (boil down/finish up/wrap up/work out) and now he's back.

3 *Complete these sentences with a verb and* **through.**

1 After many days of struggle in the jungle, the explorers finally . . . . . . into the clearing.

2 They're out celebrating — they've just . . . . . . and solved the problem that's been holding up the research.

3 Sometimes I thought she couldn't possibly survive, but she has great determination, and with the doctors' help she eventually . . . .

4 It's chaos at the moment in the office, but I expect we'll . . . . . . in the end.

5 I'm going to sneak out of the back door. Ianthe will probably ask me to her harp recital and after last time I couldn't . . . . . . another evening of it.

6 I think I'll just give up and die now — I'll never . . . . . . all this work.

4 *Answer the questions below using phrasal verbs from those discussed above and any other phrasal verbs that you can.*

1 Why couldn't the reporters get through to the area where the bomb had exploded?

2 I hear your brother's seriously ill in hospital. How is he?

3 Did you watch the late night TV movie last night?

4 Danny's a bad organizer but he always seems to get things done somehow. How does he do it?

5 What are you going to do with that pile of bricks in your garden?

119

6 There's a dangerous hole in the path by the river. What can we do about it?
7 You were going to phone Sue last night in Rome. Did you talk to her?
8 Were you caught in that heavy rain yesterday afternoon?

21 The uses of particle away

This particle has four main uses, the first being the directional use already discussed in Chapter 1. The others are as follows.

a **Away** can be used in the continuative-completive sense.

to blaze, to boil, to drink, to explain, to fire, to fritter, to gamble, to idle, to laze, to loaf, to melt, to shoot, to wear, to while

The patrol surrendered because they had *blazed/fired/shot away* until all their ammunition was finished./ The water in the kettle has *boiled away*./ He *drank/gambled/frittered away* all the money his father had left him./ The office boy found it hard to *explain away* the fact that he had been away from work when the Cup Final was being played./ The old man sat in the sun *idling/lazing* the hours *away*. Do some study, don't just *laze/loaf* your vacation *away*./ The ice on the rivers was slowly *melting away*./ The crowd lost interest and began to *melt away (fig.)*./ Rough roads will quickly *wear away* the tread on a tyre./ To *while away* the time I was waiting for the train I bought a detective novel.

Away can be used with many other verbs in this way
e.g. The students *talked, argued/smoked/drank/danced* the night *away*.

b **Away** is also used in the continuative sense, often combined with the preposition **at**. It can be used with a great number of verbs in this way. Some examples are

to beaver, to cry, to dig, to dream, to hammer, to laugh, to peg, to plug, to pound, to pull, to scrub, to slog, to talk, to tick, to work

Michael spends hours *beavering/working away* at his thesis./ The child was *crying/weeping away* in the corner./ The children are quite happy *digging away* in the sand./ Don't sit there *dreaming away* the time; go and do some work./ He *hammered/pounded away* at the door but no one came./ The boy was *laughing away* to himself./ Janet is not particularly clever but she *pegged/plugged/slogged away* at her studies and eventually got a degree./ The charwoman was *scrubbing away* at the dirty floor./ At the party Stephanie was *talking away* nineteen to the dozen./ I can hear the grandfather clock *ticking away* in the hall.

c Like **off**, **away** can be used with many verbs of cutting, forcing etc. It conveys the sense of removing an obstacle or hindrance. Examples of these verbs are

to blast, to break, to brush, to bulldoze, to chop, to cut, to dig, to hack, to knock, to pull, to push, to shovel, to slash, to strip, to sweep, to tear, to throw

A great mass of rocks fell on the road and had to be *blasted/bulldozed away*./ I managed to *break away* from the crowd./ When I held up my hand to stop him from entering he *brushed/knocked/pushed* it *away*./ When the mast fell over the ship's side the seamen had to *chop/cut/hack/slash* it *away*./ In winter you often have to *dig/shovel/sweep* the snow *away* from the front door of the house./ His mother grabbed the boy's hand but he *pulled/tore* it *away*./ There is too often a veil of official secrecy over events which is very hard to *strip away*./

d Other verbs with *away*

to be/get carried, to die, to do, to feed, to give, to hide, to stash (*coll.*), **to store, to throw**

When Jane goes to the opera she gets quite *carried away* (= overcome with emotion) by the singing./ The noise of the sirens *died away*. We must *do away* with (= get rid of) all these petty regulations./ The police suspected that he had *done away* (= murdered) with his wife./ The picture on the TV screen *faded away*./ I don't want those golf clubs; *give* them *away*./ I told him the news in confidence but he *gave* it *away* (= revealed it). The miser had a lot of money *stashed/hidden/stored away*. Those shoes are useless now; *throw* them *away*.

Exercises

1 *Complete each sentence by using one of the phrasal verbs discussed above, or any other that is appropriate. Discuss any alternatives.*

1 John is a drunkard. He never has any money. He just . . . . . . it . . . .
2 Jane just cannot keep a secret. She always . . . . . . herself . . . .
3 Barbara's hair fell over her eyes and she . . . . . . it . . . . . . with her hand.
4 The boy was . . . . . . at the piece of wood with an old, blunt saw.
5 It takes a lot of work to become a millionaire from nothing but, if you . . . . . . at it you might succeed.
6 Litter is caused by people who . . . . . . plastic bags and ice-cream cartons without thinking.
7 John was the only one who saw the joke and he sat there . . . . . . to himself.
8 Before the days of banks people used to . . . . . . their money . . . . . . in mattresses and under the floor.
9 All right Joe, calm down. I only said that you might have got the job. It's not certain yet so don't get . . . .
10 After the earthquake people were buried under tons of masonry and the rescuers had to . . . . . . it . . . . . . with their hands.
11 When Fred's wife noticed lipstick on his shirt collar he immediately started to . . . . . . it . . . .
12 Mary was left some money by her mother but she . . . . . . it . . . . . . on expensive clothes and useless jewellery.
13 With their machetes the jungle travellers . . . . . . the vines and branches that blocked their path.
14 The old lady was getting thinner and thinner. She almost seemed to be . . . .
15 The owner kept . . . . . . at the donkey's reins but the animal would not move an inch.
16 I think we could . . . . . . with a lot of these government regulations.
17 The farmers had to . . . . . . the obstruction that was blocking the irrigation channel.
18 I was woken in the middle of the night by someone . . . . . . at the front door.
19 Over centuries the abrasive action of glaciers can . . . . . . mountains . . . .
20 The banks of the river had been . . . . . . by the flood waters.

2 *Choose the correct form from those given in brackets or put an appropriate particle or verb in each space.*

1 One of the party members was (messed/closed/choked/mixed/boxed) up in a scandal and the party tried to (close/sew/hush/block/clam) it up. They forgot, however that there are reporters who have noses for smelling . . . . . . scandals no matter how carefully they are concealed and in no time the whole thing was written (off/out/down/through/up) in all the major papers. The man concerned, however, managed to brazen it (off/away/through/out/down) and now, that all the fuss has died (off/down/through/over/out), he is campaigning for a seat in parliament.

2 As you know, Miss Jones, I . . . . . . off to London early tomorrow. Please ring the agents and check (over/off/away/up/in) on my hotel reservations. At this time of the year the hotels are packed . . . . . . with tourists and I don't want to (wind/turn/set/take/pull) up and find the hotel booked . . . . Oh, and you may as well ask again what time the plane . . . . . . off.

3 Susan is such a lively person. She loves to dress up and make herself . . . . . . and go . . . . . . at night. Almost every evening some young man calls . . . . . . for her and they go . . . . . . to a dance or a party. I realise that, when you are young, you should be able to live it (off/through/over/about/up) a bit but there's no use in dancing and partying your life . . . . . . the way Susan does. I try to tell her that she ought to settle . . . . . . and do some serious study and when she's got her final examination . . . . . . she can enjoy herself again, but she just won't listen.

3 *Try to answer these questions using phrasal verbs from those discussed above and any other phrasal verbs that you can.*

1 What has happened to all the money that Fred was left by his father?
2 Is this old coat of yours of any use to you any more?
3 John always gets such good marks from his teacher for his homework. How does he do it?
4 Look at little Bobby over there by himself in the corner. What is he up to?
5 I thought that Joan's wedding was to be a secret. How is it that everyone knows about it?
6 What will happen if you forget to turn the electric kettle off?

7 What had to be done when the railway line was blocked by a fall of earth?
8 Why does Janet talk so much when she starts telling us about her children?

The uses of the particle *back*

22

Back has a directional function as discussed in Chapter 1. It has three other main uses.

a It can be used to describe position.

to lie, to stay

You've missed your train, so you might as well *lie back* and enjoy the TV play./ I *stayed back* for a few minutes to talk to Denise after the others had gone.

b **Back** is also used to describe reciprocal actions.

to call, to fire, to fight, to hit, to kick, to pay, to phone, to push, to shoot, to shout, to stare, to strike, to write

Sorry, you've phoned at an awkward moment; can I *call/phone* you *back*?/ When the police fired/shot at the robbers they *fired/shot back*./ If someone attacks you you must *fight/strike back*./ Johnny hit/kicked Billy, and unfortunately for him, Billy *hit/kicked back*./ Lend me £1.00 and I'll *pay* you *back* on Friday./ I wouldn't have been caught if Maurice hadn't informed on me. One day I'll *pay* him *back* (= get my revenge)./ If you push me, I warn you, I'll *push* you *back*./ Ian shouted at Rachel and she *shouted back* even more loudly./ He stared at me and I *stared back*./ She wrote me a letter — I must *write back*.

c **Back** can also be used to convey the idea of a repeated action. In this sense it can be used with many verbs. Some examples are

to drive, to phone, to play, to put, to shift, to start, to walk

Fred is *driving* up to London and *back* tomorrow./ I couldn't get through to him this morning so I *phoned back* later./ When I had recorded the record on the tape, I *played* the tape *back*./ If you take a book from the shelf, *put* it *back*;/ They shifted to Manchester but *shifted back* a month later./ It is getting late, we had better *start back*./ He walked to the front door then *walked back* into the living room because he had forgotten his briefcase.

d Other verbs with *back*

to cut, to fall, to hold, to set

The company muat *cut back* (= decrease) expenses. During the famine the villagers *fell back* on roots and insects. (= used in emergency)/ I was lucky. As a student I always had my family to *fall back* on./When the sergeant asked for volunteers the soldier *held back*. The bad weather *set* the construction project *back* at least two months.

1 *Complete each sentence with a suitable phrasal verb and* **back**

1 If you take a book out of the library, ... it . . . . . . on time.
2 I can't give you an answer on the phone now but I'll talk it over with my partner and . . . . . . you . . . . . . in an hour.
3 We started to run out of money in Italy and that . . . . . . our holiday plans quite a bit.
4 'That girl keeps staring at me.' 'Well you . . . . . . at her.'
5 You're not a good correspondent. I write to you but you never . . . .
6 I thought Wilkins would volunteer for the dangerous mission but he . . . . . . and someone else was chosen.
7 Oh well, even if we do both lose our jobs, we can always . . . . . . on your rich and eccentric aunt.
8 I hope the cassette recorder is recording properly. You'd better . . . . . . that concert just to make sure.

2 *Put one of these particles in each space below —* **up, down, out, over, back**

1 Don't leave the cat inside. Put it . . . . . . please.
2 We have a spare bedroom so we can put you . . . . . . when you visit England.
3 Stephen has lots of ideas for improving the firm's efficiency but he can't put them . . . .

127

4 Andrea has had my lawn mower for over three weeks, I hope she brings it . . . . . . soon.
5 Susan is always putting herself . . . . . . for other people but she doesn't get much in return.
6 That's a heavy bag you've got. Put it . . . . . . here for a minute.
7 There's an awful lot of crackling on this line. Put the phone down and I'll call you . . . .
8 We weren't doing so badly with our budget, but having to replace the alligator has set us a bit. We'll have to put the entrance fee . . . . . . again.
9 I shall never forget that it was Arthur who locked me in the refrigerating room. I shan't rest until I've paid him . . . .

3 *Answer these questions using phrasal verbs from those discussed above and any others that you can think of. Work in pairs.*

1 Have you had a letter from Jane yet?
2 What happened when little Billy kicked Adrian?
3 If you phone someone, and they are not there, what do you usually do?
4 We're likely to be completely snowed in tomorrow, and there's no fresh food in the house. What shall we do?
5 I don't want this book the Book Club have sent me. Do I have to keep it?
6 I can't possibly stay in bed today. I've got about three meetings that I mustn't miss. Curse this broken leg! What shall I do?

Answer section

1 Particles with verbs of motion

1 1 around 2 back 3 out; in 4 out; past/by/along; around 5 up 6 out 7 by; in 8 along 9 away 10 by/past; in/by

2 1 go up 2 driving down 3 went in 4 came back 5 moves down 6 moving in

3 1 fell down/over 2 driving/hurrying/walking past/by 3 climb/get up 4 walk/hurry by/past 5 bring them over/around 6 get/jump over/across 7 fell back/down 8 drive up 9 jumped back/ran away 10 ran/walked off 11 jump/climb/get in 12 get through/past

4 1 Come in!/Come on in! 2 Get out! 3 Go away and never come back. 4 You can take it away but you must bring it back. 5 I'm sorry — I'm going out. I'll be back in an hour.

2 Particles with verbs implying motion: part 1

1 1 breathe; out 2 up; see/show 3 in; help 4 hammer/drive; taking 5 sucked/pulled up 6 out; broke 7 put took/pulled it 8 in; over/around 9 up; to help; waved 10 take 11 down; be

2 1 put down 2 push up 3 ordered/called out 4 taken down 5 had in 6 waved away 7 come up 8 put/pour in

3 (Suggested answers only) 1 Because I called/beckoned him over 2 Because we asked/invited them down 3 You should go up to him and help him across. 4 Pull/take it out 5 'Ask him to sit down. I'll be out in a minute.' 6 I would show/kick/throw them out 7 You should stand up and see them out. 8 'Tell her to come up.'

3 Particles with verbs implying motion: part 2

1 1 let; up; down; out; out 2 break/get, over; down 3 up; push/force; smuggle 4 up/out; over; back; let; looked 5 looked; ship; fly 6 forces; up; down 7 threw; out 8 out; flew 9 out; phoned; past/by 10 in; washed

2 1 break 2 throw 3 force 4 sent 5 work 6 washed 7 phoned; break 8 pointing

3 (Suggested answers only) 1 I'd go up to him and question him. 2 I'd pull out the plug and let the water run away. 3 Try to wash it down with some water. 4 I had to break in/climb in through the window. 5 We railed/flew them up. 6 So that people passing/walking by can't look/see in. 7 I look up to see what is flying/passing over. 8 He might show/kick me out.

4 Particles expressing position or place

1 out; put; locked/shut 2 up; stay; down 3 by/over/around/in; in; out; in 4 held/kept; down; back; on 5 find; away/out; back 6 walked out; are out; stay out 7 going away; be away; flying over/across; driving down 8 get on; stay on; get off; hold your hat on; blow off

2 (Suggested answers only) 1 I'd lock/shut him out. 2 I held him back 3 They left it in. 4 To hold the tent down. 5 To hold the tent up. 6 No, I'd stay in. 7 I'm sorry but he's out/away. 8 He falls down and stays down.

5 *Off* with verbs of motion and verbs implying motion

1 1 clear 2 made 3 are 4 set 5 rode

2 1 kicked/bullied 2 started/set; sent 3 on; rode; back; up 4 takes; set/start; take; get off 5 up; away; drift; started; around; back 6 getting; getting; see; goes; back; take/drive 7 down; mail/send; get 8 sent/mailed; back; off 9 blasted/lifted; up;

3 (Suggested answers only) 1 Before I could look around he had run away. 2 I'd turn around and make/run off/run away. 3 I'll set/start off very early. 4 They're off! 5 Because the plane takes off at 8.30 a.m. 6 I'm going to mail/send them off and hope that some replies will come back. 7 They are kicking off at 3 p.m. 8 I'm sorry I have to hurry off. 9 We should go and see them off. 10 When he came out he was whisked off in an official car.

4 1 marched off 2 flew off 3 step/start off 4 swam off 5 set/started off 6 ran off 7 carried off 8 send off; walked off 9 blast/lift off 10 sets/starts off; see off

6 *About* and *around* with verbs of motion

1 down; crowded/gathered; help her up; through; out; up 2 turned/spun; off/away; off; away; walked/looked 3 off; fly/circle; down; over/across; standing 4 in; out; gets 5 in; in; off; walking/wandering; blown 6 up; wandering/walking; up; off; in 7 back; put/go down; swimming; up 8 in; wandering/prowling; off

2 1 wander 2 flitting 3 dashing 4 get; stroll 5 moving 6 blown 7 gathered 8 circling

3 (Suggested answers only) 1 I'd put/go about and sail back. 2 They crowd around and have to be told to stand back. 3 I turn/spin around. 4 He staggers/reels about/around and sometimes falls down and can't get up. 5 They jump/run about/around. 6 He wants to get out and walk about/around in the open air. 7 They like to watch them swimming about/around. 8 They get out of bed and walk about/around.

7 *About* and *around* with other verbs

1 1 tossed 2 loaf 3 fish 4 kicking 5 look 6 knock 7 gazed 8 be

2 1 out; hang/wait/sit 2 fishing; wait/hang; get off 3 up; down; fishing/feeling/wandering; order/push 4 strolling/walking; sitting/lazing about; about/around 5 sit/hang/loaf; out; ask/invite; out; knock/hit; loafing/hanging/sitting 6 standing/waiting/hanging; out; waiting/standing/hanging; out; off/away; off 7 off; off; spread 8 shop; went; off; staring/gazing/looking; stood; stand/wait

3 (Suggested answers only) 1 They stand around/about and gaze about/around. 2 I fish around/about for it. 3 You can swap/change it about/around. 4 You'll have to go out and shop around. 5 They like to laze/loaf around/about in the sun; knock a golf ball about etc. 6 They think they can push them around/about. 7 I'd take him about/around to see the sights; take him up to London etc. 8 I would go/set about clearing up the mess.

4 1 off; down 2 around; out 3 around; down 4 off; about; off 5 off; about; down 6 away; out; around; out; over; in 7 about; in; in; around 8 around; off; back

5 1 knocked; playing/fooling; down 2 down; out; about/around; off/away 3 up; back; off; away/off; off/away 4 away; down; thrown/tossed; about; sail/go/get; down; about/around 5 in; about/around; off; kick/throw; out 6 down; up; be about; in; in

6 (Suggested answers only) 1 Some were running around, others were pottering about with toy boats. 2 She fell down yesterday and knocked herself out. 3 He messes/potters about with his car engine. 4 We hung about in the passenger lounge until the plane took off. 5 He was riding/fooling/messing about/around on his bicycle and he fell off. 6 They think they can push them about/around./They think they can keep them waiting/hanging/about/around for hours. 7 Sometimes they like to go away and knock around/about for a few years. 8 They like to sit/laze about in the sun. They like to potter about.

8 *Off* expressing the completive aspect of the verb

1 1 round; is off 2 off; 2 off; down; off 3 about; off; about; down; off 4 off; about; away; 5 about; off; out; 6 around; out; off; off

2 1 tossed 2 dozed 3 paid 4 written 5 called 6 die 7 fight 8 come 9 came; leave 10 pull; finished 11 knock; cool; dry 12 set;

3 (Suggested answers only) 1 I'd tell him to knock off and I'd invite him over to have a few beers. 2 I put them in and they came up all right but the dry weather is killing them off. 3 It usually drops/dozes off. 4 It was called off. 5 Because he wanted to dry his clothes off. 6 They threw them down on their enemies to try to hold/fight them off. 7 I hope you can pull it off/I hope it comes off all right.

9 *Up* expressing the completive aspect of the verb: part 1

1 wrap up 2 closed/shut 3 silted up 4 plugged/sealed/stopped it up 5 cooped up 6 blocked/clogged/closed up 7 clutter up 8 sew them up 9 button it up 10 buckle up 11 bricked/closed/sealed up 12 pack up 13 packed up 14 cooped 15 tied/wrapped/sewn up

2 1 about; pack/parcel/wrap; off 2 silted; down 3 bricked/sealed; fall 4 out; wrap; back 5 stuffed; cooped; about/around 6 lock/shut/close; out; in; out 7 about; tightened 8 about/around; cooped/caged 9 locked; off 10 fed; cooped/shut; out

3 (Suggested answers only) 1 I can hardly get in as it's so cluttered up with sports gear. 2 I don't like to see animals caged up with nothing to do but lie about/around 3 The pipe is probably blocked/clogged up. 4 Well you can't go out like that — you'll have to get it sewn up. 5 Whenever I go out there are thousands of people moving about. I am cooped up in buses and trains. It makes me so fed up. 6 Tighten them up. 7 Rivers are dammed up. The water flows down large pipes etc. 8 I usually wrap them up in coloured paper, then tie them up with red ribbon. 9 I wrap myself up well and I don't stay out very long. 10 I bend down and I tie them up.

10 *Up* expressing the completive sense of the verb: part 2:

1 1 splitting 2 piled 3 washed 4 round 5 dug 6 piling 7 sweep 8 belt 9 mess them 10 make herself

2 1 clean; raked/swept; piled; ploughed 2 clean; round 3 cut; breaking 4 messed; making myself 5 clean/tidy; sweep; wash 6 smarten 7 messed/fouled/screwed; clam 8 rake; shut 9 dressed/togged; mess/foul/muck/screw 10 rake; clammed/ buttoned

3 (Suggested answers only) 1 You should dig up those weeds, pile them up and burn them. Then you should dig up the ground and put in some new plants. 2 First you can clean up your own room. Then you can sweep up the mess on this floor. 3 Please pick them up and put them back on the shelf or I'll bundle them up and throw them out. 4 The dance is off. Sue messed/mucked up the arrangements. 5 They were dug up somewhere in Greece 6 She was driving along the other day and the car skidded and crashed. It's been written off. 7 He told him to belt up. 8 She loves to get dressed up in her best clothes. 9 She has been rather cut up lately as she thinks her marriage is breaking up. 10 Yes, I think I can rake up the money.

4 1 mixed 2 freezes 3 roughed; ganged 4 swallowed 5 saving 6 rounded 7 jumbled 8 split; settle 9 reckoning; tot them 10 measure

5 1 snowed; wrap 2 treasured 3 mix 4 eat 5 roughed/beaten; ganged 6 sealed/bricked/closed 7 wrapped/sewn/tied 8 mixed 9 froze; reckoned 10 add

6 1 off; up; up; around; back 2 up; about/around; up 3 up; up; off 4 about/around; up; in 5 in; up; out; up; up 6 out; up; out;

up; up   7 up; off; away; away; up   8 off; on; across/over; back; up

7   1 I dislike it when everything snows/freezes up. I don't like having to wrap myself up whenever I go out.   2 They have to save up, pay a deposit and then pay the rest off.   3 We usually cage them up and fatten them up.   4 First of all measure up the floor and the walls. Then reckon up the cost.   5 They pull them about/around and chew them up.   6 They frost/freeze up and get clogged up with ice.

11   Other common verbs used with *up*

1   1 playing/acting; gave   2 is; hurry   3 check; buy   4 fed; came, cropped   5 give; finish/end   6 give; blow   7 bottle; bolstered/built him   8 blow herself; grown   9 ended/finished; back him   10 following; end/finish

2   1 coming/shooting; off; give; put   2 about/around; out/up; up; over/around   3 up; off; up; work;   4 grew; building/bolstering; off; let   5 down; blow; off; down   6 tidy/clean; up; about/around; up; going; back; in; out; cooped   7 up; up; come; up; give   8 fed; up; off/away; saved; over/across; rake

3   (Suggested answers only)   1 You sometimes get fed up but you mustn't give up. Keep trying and you will finish/end up a success.   2 You should take down those old curtains and put up some new ones. You should paint up some of that old furniture etc.   3 Wrap yourself up well and button up your collar. Keep moving about/around or your feet will freeze up.   4 Would you mind parcelling them up and mailing them off for me?   5 Why don't you belt up and push off?   6 I think they should be sealed up because if children go in they may not be able to get out.   7 They like to dress themselves up and make themselves up nicely.   8 Rescuers have given up hope for the crew of the ship that broke up on the coast yesterday.

4   1 wind up; take up   2 took up; make it up   3 set up; sell up   4 living it up; hushed up   5 make up; wound/keyed up   6 woke up; open that up   7 loosens me up; wind up   8 making it up; own up   9 pull up; made up; pay up   10 written up; summed up

5   1 up; about/around   2 off; up   3 about/around; up; off;   4 up; off; to up; up; up   5 off; about/around; up   6 about/around; up; up   7 up; about/around; up   8 up; mail off; about/around; up; off

6   1 acting; pack   2 dress; make   3 cut; broke   4 drink; belt   5

locked; wind   6 hush; written   7 give; bolstering   8 bashed   9 open her; wind up   10 fed; bottling things; build

7 (Suggested answers only)   1 I'd give up my job.   I'd live it up a bit. I'd take up golf and yachting.   2 When I get up I like to loosen up a bit.   3 You have to sell up all your stock to pay off your debts.   4 Go up and wake her up. If she won't get up, pull her out.   5 No, I think he makes them up.   6 I feel all wound/keyed up.   7 They try to hush it up.   8 The best thing to do is to own up.   9 I'd take him up on it.   10 I put up in a small hotel. Sometimes I camp out.

12   The use of the particle *down*

1 up; up; nailed   2 boils up; close/shut; up   3 bogged; back   4 breaking; up   5 stuck; calm/cool/simmer   6 up; calm   7 tied; about/around   8 off; pinned   9 breaks   10 up; out/off; nailed/glued/tied; damp   11 died; settled

2 1 down; about/around   2 down; out   3 up; down; up   4 down; about/around; up   5 off; down; down; up; down; up; up; down   7 up; down; off; up; out   8 off; up; up; about/around; off; down

3 (Suggested answers only)   1 Wrap/parcel them up. Tie them up well. Take them around to the post office. Mail them off.   2 I might get bogged down. I'd have to hose/wash it down/wipe off the dirt.   3 We set off late. Then the car broke down. We got there and put the tents up but they weren't pegged down properly. In the night they fell down.   4 They wind/end up by having a break-down. They have to knock off work.   5 You can nail it down/screw it down.   6 They are selling off some stock to bring in some money. Perhaps they have debts to pay off. Perhaps they are closing down.   7 If you keep your premium paid up and your house burns down you may get enough money to pull the damaged house down and put up a new one.   8 The best thing is to stop arguing, go away and simmer/calm/cool down.   9 The authorities will clamp down on them.   10 You can't knock about/around any longer. You may be tied down by a family. There's little chance to live it up.

4 1 nestled; off   2 wiped; down   3 torn; put   4 up; blown; kill   5 runs; build   6 give; pin   7 up; settled; live; turned   8 clammed; down; owned   9 fed; down; rise; put   10 building; down; up

5 1 belt/shut up   2 bottle up   3 fight down   4 put down   5 living it up   6 shouted him down   7 broke down   8 gave up   9 glued down   10 clamp down on; bogged down   11 pulled/torn down;

put up   12 tumble down   13 knocking/wandering about/around; settle down   14 track it down   15 burnt down; cut up

6 (Suggested answers only)   1 We should make them sit or lie down quietly until they calm down.   2 A lot of people stood up, waved their arms about and shouted him down.   3 I put out my hand and, if it's cold, I pull the blankets up, snuggle/nestle down and drop/doze off again.   4 He's settled down and is trying to live down his past life.   5 She called the last meeting off and I can't pin/tie her down to a date for the next. She tends to mess/muck things up a bit.   6 I piled it up yesterday and it's been written off. The broken-down old thing was about to pack up anyway.   7 They have a lot of debts to pay off. To bring in money they sell off all their goods. They try to settle up what they owe.   8 They may mess up the place with cigarette ends and ash. If they drop/doze off while smoking in bed they may burn the house down.

13   The use of the particles, *in* and *out* to denote inclusion and exclusion

1   1 count me out   2 cut/freeze out   3 take in   4 cut/deal in   5 chickens out   6 pitch in/dig in   7 cut out   8 scrape in   9 opt out   10 written/pencilled it in   11 join in   12 get in on

2   1 in; down; down; in; up; out; in; up; up; in; up   2 down; down; out; up   3 up; down; up; down   4 in; in; out; up; up; up; up; up   5 up; down; up; up; down; down; up; down; down; down; up; down; down; out

3   1 count   2 ruled   3 phased   4 want   5 muscle   6 rope   7 pitched   8 be

4   1 horn/muscle in on   2 chickened out   3 paint in   4 scrape in   5 join in   6 'eft out   7 phase it out   8 pencil in

5 (Suggested answers only)   1 I should join in.   2 I've already made up my mind; you can count me in. I can't wait to get in on some real money.   3 You can count me out. I don't want to wind/end/finish up in gaol.   4 You can count me in.   5 I'd like to play too; can I join in?   6 Well, it takes in other subjects such as geology.   7 He had made up his mind to come but he opted out at the last minute. I think that the way the papers wrote up that climbing accident made him chicken out.   8 I think he's trying to cut Bill out. Bill won't put up with that for long.   9 Someone has messed/mucked up the arrangements and left my name out. I'll write it in now.   10 Well the voters almost kicked him out; but he just scraped in.

14 Further uses of the particles *in* and *out*

1 1 find her in 2 dined/ate out 3 kept me in 4 camped/slept out 5 stay out

2 1 closed/shut in 2 bunched/boxed in 3 belted/buckled/strapped in 4 wall/fence/it in 5 hemmed in

3 1 handed/passed/gave out 2 farms out 3 hire out 4 mete/dole out 5 sent out 6 putting out

4 1 out; closed/shut up 2 hemmed/shut; in 3 hire; down; put 4 out; made; in; up; up 5 out; backed 6 handed; make; up; end/finish/wind; out 7 up; taken about/around; dug; in; up; down; end/finish/wind 8 make; down; bogged

5 1 stay away 2 stayed out 3 stay around 4 stay down 5 stay in

6 1 taken down 2 took me about/around 3 took out 4 take his family in 5 taking off

7 (Suggested answers only) 1 Yes, we lived it up a bit. We dined out at that new restaurant. 2 I wouldn't like to be shut/hemmed in by mountains. Sometimes the people are snowed in. 3 In a day or so I'll plant them out. I've dug up some ground at the back and I'll put them in there. 4 Let's go out. Why don't we eat out somewhere, go to the theatre and finish up by going to a night club? 5 I was cooped up in one room. Now I know how animals feel when they are caged up in the zoo. 6 They'd probably farm it out or they might stop taking in any more orders. 7 Luckily I live in and I can eat in too. Sometimes for a change, however, I eat out. 8 There's no use in standing about/around on street corners holding them out to passers-by. You'll have to go around from house to house and hand them out to people. 9 A lot of holiday-makers come down here in the summer and I think he hires them out. 10 Well fold them up, put them in envelopes and send them out/off.

15 Verbs used with the particle *out* in the completive sense

1 1 black/pass out 2 sold out 3 was out 4 blotted out 5 conk out 6 fizzled out 7 buy him out 8 marked/measured out 9 straighten you out 10 ironed/smoothed out 11 packed/crowded out 12 hammer something out 13 pace it out 14 beaten/hammered out 15 mapped out

2 1 set off; finished up 2 was away; be back 3 lived it up; settled down 4 run down; wind it up 5 slow down; speed up 6 join in; opted out 7 put up; torn down 8 drop off; wakes up 9

loosened up; tightened up   10 cross my name out; write Janet's name in

3 (Suggested answers only) 1 The house would be blacked out. We'd be wandering about in the dark.   2 It was a wash-out. Too many players were sent off. From the time they kicked off no one seemed to want to win.   3 Sometimes whole areas freeze up. Fogs blot everything out. Runways are iced up.   4 We went along early but it was sold out.   5 I put out my cigarette; I turn out the lights. I snuggle down.   6 So that if they find any problems they can iron them out. They sum up its performance.   7 They marked out a court in the yard where they could throw a ball about/around.   8 They try to freeze them out. They try to muscle in on their business. They try to buy them out.   9 He started off enthusiastically, but his enthusiasm fizzled out. Now the arrangements are all messed/mucked up   10 I made up my mind to bake a cake but I found I had run out of flour.

4 1 caught   2 died   3 sort   4 run   5 missed   6 find   7 blown   8 ironed   9 stamp   10 borne   11 worked   12 drowned

5 1 up, up; make; mixed; send; about/around; up; tired; bear; in; carry; make; dine/eat   2 blocked/clogged; out; off; make; about; out/away; fed; up; tired/worn; up; out; off/away; mess; up; out

6 1 find out   2 spell them out   3 work it out   4 packed/crowded out   5 blacked out   6 drowned out   7 cancel out   8 beat/put out   9 died out   10 sorting out   11 fizzled out

7 (Suggested answers only)   1 I can't work it out. I'm fed up with it but I won't give up yet.   2 You'll end up by being found out.   3 They died out thousands of years ago.   4 You must put it out properly or stub it out otherwise you might burn the place down.   5 To see that the laws are carried out. To stamp out crime. To clamp down on law-breakers   6 Take them out, sort them out properly and put them back.   7 It has been sold out/booked up for months.   8 He has to carry it out.   8 I tried to book in there but the place was packed out with tourists.   9 Perhaps they've run out of petrol. They've broken down.

16   Further uses of the particle *out*

1 1 out; up; out; held; ferreting; hidden; out   2 off; away; down; out; out; up; out; out; have; down   3 up; up; down; up; held; work/pan; up; out; up; up; off; tired/worn; down; last; out; out; up; up; in

2 1 held   2 thought   3 worn   4 fathom   5 last   6 brazen

3 1 off 2 off 3 up 4 up 5 in; out 6 up 7 up 8 out 9 up 10 in 11 off 12 in; off

4 1 brazen it out 2 last it out 3 blow itself out 4 thrash/fight/sort it out 5 root/stamp out 6 have it out 7 reason it out 8 counted out

5 1 out 2 down 3 out 4 off 5 down 6 down

6 (Suggested answers only) 1 I feel worn/tired out. My muscles tighten up. I doze off in my chair. 2 Call a friend over, sit down and reason/thrash/think it out. 3 So that their representatives can sit down and iron/smooth out problems that come up from time to time. 4 I wouldn't give up. I'd ferret it out 5 Some decided to shoot it out. Some tried to get away. Some gave up. 6 You have to winkle it out of him. 7 They try to brazen it out. They make up excuses. Some break down and cry. 8 They are holding out for 12%. The cost of living has gone up. They have been ground down. 9 The ones he has are worn out. 10 They got away without being pursued and they must have hidden out somewhere. It was a well thought out robbery.

17 Uses of the particle *over*

1 1 fell over 2 bowled over 3 iced over 4 get it over with 5 chew/mull/think over 6 get my message over 7 blown/passed over 8 run/go over 9 boil over 10 brimmed over 11 do it all over 12 take over her class

2 1 down; fed; about; take over; be over 2 keyed; break out; was over; calmed; away 3 set/started out; iced/frozen over; up; slow; misting over; up; down 4 taken over; made; stay; start all over; blows over 5 was over; settle; found; tied; off; up; off; was over; set/started out; paid

3 1 get over it 2 got over it 3 get it over 4 got over it 5 get it over

4 1 pushed over 2 think/chew it over 3 take over 4 be over 5 was left over 6 carried over

5 1 over 2 out 3 out 4 down 5 up 6 out 7 down 8 out

6 (Suggested answers only) 1 Sit down, think it over to find out what you have done wrong and make up your mind to do it better next time. 2 Make up your mind to do it quickly and get it over with. 3 It might boil over and mess up your cooker. 4 No, the plane comes down in Singapore and I might stop over for a couple of nights. You know, put up in a good hotel and live it up a bit. 5 Don't make up your mind quickly; chew/mull/think it over first.

Sit down and reason it out. 6 It's a bird crying/calling out. It's someone's radio blaring out 7 They burst out laughing and jumped about/around in their seats. 8 A war has broken out in the Middle East. Twenty cars have piled up on the motorway. A large building was burnt down. 9 The sky has clouded over. The clouds have come down very low. 10 You have to get your information over/across.

18 the uses of *on* and *off* to convey attachment and detachment

1 1 on; blown 2 hits; cut 3 force; jammed/stuck; screw/get; hit/force 4 come/fall, screwed/jammed 5 in; out; take/slip; put/slip; up; off 6 bashed; pull/force/get 7 out; pin 8 put; up; down; over; up 9 screwed/forced; get/screw; saw/cut 10 come/fallen; sew 11 out; catch 12 knocked/kicked; glue/stick; come/fall 13 away; over/across; latch on 14 dressed up; put that on; turned up 15 burning off; broke out; beat it out

2 1 up 2 out 3 out 4 up 5 off 6 off

3 1 down 2 off 3 up 4 up 5 down 6 out

4 (Suggested answers only) 1 Someone had forced it on and it wouldn't come off. It was jammed on. 2 It's hard to hit it off with the local people. Some people feel cut off from city life. You can't live it up in a small town. 3 The handle has come/fallen off. I'll have to break it down. 4 He was walking along with his gun when he tripped over. The gun went off and he blew/shot off one of his toes. 5 He tore off his coat, dived in and dragged the child back to the river bank. 6 'No, profits have fallen off. I may have to sell out. The big supermarkets are cutting/freezing us small men out' 7 Saw some off one end then get a plane and plane it down. 8 Perhaps the electricity is off. Maybe someone turned/switched it off. Perhaps it has frosted up or broken down. It's old and it's conked out. 9 Slide it on carefully. Don't force it on. 10 They cut his head off.

5 1 railed/roped/sealed off 2 railed/roped off; put up; slow down 3 on; spill/come out 4 cooped up; curtained/partitioned off 5 wiped out; came/out 6 close/shut off; get over 7 gave up; came off 8 messing up; turns out

19 The use of *on* to express the constructive aspect of the verb

1 1 up; drag/wear, over; up; down; hold/hang; up; fall. 2 carries/ goes; latches; go; away; talks away; up 3 Come; down; off; on; up; getting; out. 4 up; get along; kick; down; away; over; out; along over; back; along; over; up 5 come; get; about/around; away; up; up; away; about/around; get; up; down; up; off; hold/ hang; up; carry

2 1 hold/hang on 2 went/dragged on (and on) 3 getting on 4 carry/go on 5 push on 6 coming on 7 soldier/battle on 8 carries on 9 going on

3 (Suggested answers only) 1 It depends upon what's on. Some films I just can't sit through. Sometimes I walk out. Sometimes I doze/ drop off. 2 I'm sick of standing about/around listening to stupid people go on about themselves. They latch on to you and talk on and on. I want to tell them to belt up. 3 I'll just hold on, sit it out and see what happens. If I soldier on and measure up to what they want, I might be able to carry on. 4 He talked it over with the manager but in the end he was turned down. 5 I have a lot of work to get through and part of the meeting was carried over until tomorrow so I have things to finish up. If I carry on I'll be through in a couple of hours. 6 It just dragged on (and on). I almost dropped off. 7 We set out after lunch. Then the rain started to pour down. We got wet through. Then the sun came out and we dried off. We walked on for several miles and sat down by a small stream.

20 The use of the particle *through*

1 1 off 2 out 3 about/around 4 over 5 off 6 out 7 out 8 over 9 through 10 through about/around

2 1 carry out 2 playing up 3 broke down 4 call off 5 hit it off 6 take over 7 sewn up 8 work out

3 1 broke/won through 2 broken through 3 pulled through 4 muddle through 5 sit through 6 get through

4 (Suggested answers only) 1 The police had cordoned/sealed it off. They were looking for clues that they might follow up. 2 The doctors think he'll pull through. They haven't given up hope. 3 Yes, I stayed up and managed to sit through it but when it was over I didn't know what it was all about. It was a real wash-out. 4 He never sits down and thinks things out first. He just starts off quite happily and seems to be able to muddle through. 5 I'm going to wall off the end of our garden. My wife and I like to lie about/around in the sun but we don't like all the neighbours looking in. 6 I think it should be railed off or someone will fall in and injure himself. Children often play around there too. 7 Yes, I got through but we were drowned out by a lot of noise. Anyway she's going to ring me back 8 Yes, I had just set off for work when it began to pour down. I got wet through and it took me a couple of hours to dry my clothes off.

21   The uses of the particle, *away*

1   1 drinks it away   2 gives herself away   3 brushed it away   4 sawing away   5 peg/plug/slog/work away at it   6 throw away   7 laughing away   8 stash/hide/put their money away   9 carried away   10 tear/pull it away   11 explain it away   12 frittered it away   13 cut/slashed away   14 fading away   15 pulling/jerking away   16 do away with   17 clear/dig away   18 banging/bashing/belting/pounding away   19 wear mountains away   20 washed/carried/worn away by the flood waters.

2   1 mixed up in; hush it up; smelling out; written up; brazen it out; died down/away   2 am/go off; check up on; packed out; turn up; booked up; takes off   3 make herself up; go out; calls around; go out/off; live it up; partying your life away; settle down; got her examination over

3   (Suggested answers only)   1 What he didn't drink and gamble away he frittered away on cars and clothes. He has gone through it all now.   2 No, it's almost worn out. It won't last through the winter. Throw it out or give it away   3 He doesn't loaf/idle his time away. He plugs/slogs away at his work. He beavers away at his books.   4 He is playing away with his toy cars. He'll mess about/around like that for hours. He does not seem to join in when the other children play.   5 Well, one of her friends blurted it out and others spread it about/around. I think that even Joan herself gave the secret away.   6 The water will boil over. The water will boil away and the element might burn out.   7 It had to be dug/bulldozed away so that the train could get through.   8 She likes to build them up and she gets carried away. She doesn't know when to shut up.

22 The particle *back*

1 1 take back 2 call/ring/phone back 3 set back 4 stare back 5 write back 6 held back 7 fall back 8 play back

2 1 out 2 up 3 over 4 back 5 out 6 down 7 back 8 back; up 9 back

3 (suggested answers only) 1 I wrote but she hasn't written back. I'm through with her. 2 Adrian kicked him back. Billy knocked Adrian down. Adrian cried out for his mother. 3 I usually hold on for a while and then decide to phone/ring/call them back. 4 We can fall back on tinned food and if it stops snowing we can dig our way out and go down to the village. 5 No, you can send it back, they can't make you hold on to it. 6 Well there's not much you can do about it so you may as well lie back and relax. I can go to the meetings if you like, and report back. Calm down!